THE STARVING ARTIST'S SURVIVAL GUIDE

By Marianne Taylor and Laurie Lindop

Illustrated by Paul Weil

SIMON SPOTLIGHT ENTERTAINMENT
New York London Toronto Sydney

This book is dedicated to
Ellen Abdow, Henry Barbaro, and Lucy Lyons.

SIMON SPOTLIGHT ENTERTAINMENT

An imprint of Simon & Schuster

1230 Avenue of the Americas, New York, New York 10020

Text copyright © 2005 by Marianne Taylor and Laurie Lindop

Illustrations copyright © 2005 by Paul Weil

SIMON SPOTLIGHT ENTERTAINMENT and related logo are trademarks of
Simon & Schuster, Inc.

Designed by Yaffa Jaskoll and Greg Stadnyk

Manufactured in the United States of America

First Edition 10 9 8 7 6 5 4 3 2 1

Library of Congress Cataloging-in-Publication Data

Taylor, Marianne, 1962–

The starving artist's survival guide / by Marianne Taylor and Laurie Lindop ;
illustrated by Paul Weil.— 1st ed.

p. cm.

Includes bibliographical references.

ISBN-13: 978-1-4169-0826-5

ISBN-10: 1-4169-0826-9

1. Authorship—Humor. 2. Art—Humor. I. Lindop, Laurie. II. Title.

PN6231.A77T39 2005

818'.607—dc22

2005012962

CONTENTS

CHAPTER FIVE:
ARTISTIC STYLE

CHAPTER SIX:
ARTISTIC RELATIONSHIPS

CHAPTER SEVEN:
ENDING IT ALL

NOTES

ACKNOWLEDGMENTS

We would like to thank our agent, Ted Gideonse; our editor, Patrick Price; the illustrator, Paul Weil; and the S&S designers Russell Gordon, Yaffa Jaskoll, and Greg Stadnyk.

And finally, we would like to thank the starving poet Don Colburn, who when we called to tell him we wanted to publish his poem "In the Workshop," rejoiced: "You didn't just make my day, or my month, but my entire year!"

INTRODUCTION

On a gloomy November night, we sat moping over our usual table at the Wonder Spice Café. One of us had just been rejected by the MacDowell Colony and the other's agent had told her it was time to "put the novel in the drawer for a year or two," which was obviously code for "I'm tired of circulating this piece of shit."

While listlessly moving pad Thai around our plates, we began the slow and all-too-familiar process of ego repair:

"Like your agent really knows the market anyway."

"MacDowell is for pretentious sad sacks—you're too good for MacDowell."

"My novel is apparently 'too quirky.'"

"You know what sells out there?"

"Yeah, bathroom facts and chicken soup—nonfiction, that's what really sells."

And then there was silence for a very long time.

"Imagine writing nonfiction?"

Silence again.

"But you gotta know about stuff."

"We know some stuff."

A thoughtful silence.

"What about a book all about rejection and humiliation?"

"No chicken soup, though."

"Yeah, something that dejected artists wouldn't choke on."

"It would be like . . . these dinners, but in a book."

And so we wrote it. Our fabulous *new* agent, Ted, jumped up and down on the subway when he read it. Ted likes quirky, as does our discerning editor, Patrick. So there.

Trust us, this is writing from the front lines. Between us, we have racked up hundreds of rejections and feigned delight at the success of our brethren. We have slept in closets, eaten falafels for weeks on end, and haven't been to the dentist since the Clinton administration. We understand the fine line between artistic integrity and out-and-out depravity: It is perhaps best expressed by the speech that struggling actor Michael Dorsey (Dustin Hoffman) gives in the movie *Tootsie*. Once his agent tells him he's unhireable, Michael Dorsey begins to shout about how he had played a stand-up tomato. "Nobody does vegetables like me!" He points out that he did a whole evening of vegetables Off Broadway. "I did a tomato, a cucumber, an endive salad that knocked the critics on their ass!"

Michael Dorsey needed a book like ours. Unemployed, in his tomato suit, he could have made a Toilet Paper Effigy of his agent (page 6). He could have fashioned his own glowing review filling in our interactive exercise (page 52). That would have made him feel better. So don't despair if you find yourself sweating in a hot dog suit handing out fliers. Go home, flop down on your garbage-picked mattress, and crack open this book.

CHAPTER ONE

REJECTION

We hear it all the time: how rejection is part of the artistic process, how we must come to accept, even grow from, our failures—well, screw that. Rejection feels rotten because it is rotten. How rotten? Well, that depends on the type of letter. Some rejection letters are more insulting than others.

The Don't Even Bother: slip form, quarter sheet of paper, unsigned

> The manuscript submitted does not fit our current editorial needs. Due to the high number of submissions received, we request you do not send us future work.
>
> The Editorial Assistant

The Brush-off: form letter, full-page

> We appreciate your interest in the magazine, but unfortunately were unable to accept your work

for publication. We wish you luck in placing it elsewhere.

As you know, our literary magazine publishes the best up-and-coming fiction, poetry, and groundbreaking memoirs. If you subscribe today, we offer one free back issue and 30 percent off the current rate.

Best Regards,
The Editorial Staff

The Apologetic Diss: form letter, signed

Thank for you submitting your manuscript _____. We regret we are unable to publish your work. Our selection process is highly subjective; we may publish only one out of the hundreds of submissions we receive each issue.

We're aware that writing is hard work and writers merit some acknowledgment. While we realize a form letter doesn't speak to that need, please know that we appreciate your interest in our magazine.

(signed)
The Editor

The Editorial Bone: form letter with encouraging personal note (same as above with added handwritten missive)

> While I enjoyed the narrator's nail-biting predicament, I was disappointed when the entire story turned out to be a drug-induced Vietnam flashback.

The Call Your Mama (or The Big Nirvana?): handwritten with request for more work or rewrite

> Wow! What a story. The flashback twist really caught me by surprise. Although "Bloody Laundry" in its current form is not quite right for our magazine, I found the protagonist beguiling, if somewhat unbelievable. Please send other work, perhaps something more uplifting, or a less graphic version of "Bloody."
>
> Please keep us in mind,
> The Editor

Your average artist amplifies the suffering by reading the rejection letter again and again. With highlighter in hand, the rejected emblazons each incriminating adjective. To the old adage, "What doesn't kill you makes you stronger," we say, "Poppycock!" What doesn't kill you makes you feel like shit for weeks on end. At this point, it's time to pump that destructive self-pity into creative action.

FUN WITH REJECTION AND TOILET PAPER

The following activities have been used in various psychiatric hospitals, prisons, nursing homes, and other ill-fated institutions. It has long been known that trivial craft projects deflect the agony of the dark-hearted and cynical. The goal here is not to make great art but to create a purpose, an actual need, for your rejection letters.

TOILET PAPER EFFIGY

Pick your nemesis: agent, editor, director, curator, critic. Effigies say "Die, motherfucker" better than any vengeful threat or dartboard. You will need: scissors, glue, a photo (or a copy of one) of your nemesis, a cardboard toilet paper tube, a Ping-Pong ball, a rejection letter, and lighter fluid.

1. Paste your rejection letter around the cardboard tube. Trim excess.

2. Make two slits opposite each other in the toilet paper tube. The cuts should go a third of the way up the tube.

3. Curve each of the two flaps you just created into small cylinders—these will be the legs.

4. Glue the Ping-Pong ball into the top of the tube.

5. Paste an image of your nemesis's face onto the Ping-Pong ball (or simply draw your own rendition).

6. Douse in lighter fluid and burn on fire escape.

PAPER CHAIN NOOSE

This one's easy. Create one for every room. You will need: many rejection letters, scissors, and stapler.

1. Cut rejection letters in half, then into strips.

2. Staple one loop, then create another inside the first, staple, and repeat continuously.

3. Hang chain from ceiling. Loop into noose.

GOLD MACARONI FRAME

Here's a great way to display your all-time favorite! You will need: your best (i.e., most insulting) rejection letter, glue, dry macaroni, foam- or cardboard, and gold or silver spray paint.

1. Paste macaroni shapes to the edges of a ten-by-twelve inch piece of cardboard or foamboard. You may want to alternate your pasta shape with bow ties, rotini, and wagon wheels for a thoughtfully patterned design.

2. Coat with gold spray paint (or use silver for a more industrial look).

3. Glue rejection letter inside your gorgeous frame and hang it on wall for all to marvel at.

HOLIDAY ARSON BALLS

This a delightful holiday treat if you're one of the few artists lucky enough to have a fireplace. If not, an alley garbage can will do. Grab your friends and a few gallons of eggnog, and let the fun begin. You will need: potpourri (or substitute dead flowers and crushed pine needles), cheap bourbon, festive ribbons, and rejection letters.

1. Place rejection letter facedown and plunk a handful of potpourri onto its center.

2. Fold up corners and gather at the top like a doggie bag.

3. Cinch with festive ribbon.

4. Douse in cheap bourbon and toss into the fire.

ANGEL OF DESPAIR

Why not pray *while* sobbing on your knees? Remove your hands from in front of your face and clasp them together before this lovely Angel of Despair. You will need: scissors, glue, your favorite rejection letter, poster board, paper doily, and metal beer pull tab.

1. Back your rejection letter by gluing it to a piece of stiffer poster board.

2. Cut letter into the biggest half circle it can make.

3. Fold half circle into cone and glue at seams.

4. Trace hand shape onto two doilies and cut out.

5. Glue doilies to back of cone to create wings.

6. Draw head and arms on poster board and cut out. Attach to cone body with glue.

7. Glue beer pull tab to head to create halo.

SASE AFFIRMATIONS

Nothing is worse than a mailbox full of your own SASEs. Rarely does an acceptance letter come back in the Self-Addressed-Stamped-Envelope you sent in with your feeble submission. When you open your mailbox and see them stacked in there, the artistic ego begins to deflate instantly. A nice thing to do to alleviate the pain is to write tiny affirmations along the back flap of your envelopes—things like "I am a child of the universe," or "I can still have a fabulous day!" or "Fuck me!"

OUR FAVORITE REJECTION HAIKUS

Skipping to mailbox
Find my own SASE
Rot, editor, rot.

You, blinking red light,
A callback from my agent?
No, just goddamn Mom.

Simultaneous submissions
Aren't allowed, but you do it
And never get caught.

The Prize Issue comes
From contest you lost. Screw them.
Return to sender.

Please don't call us 'cause
We'll call you. Ha, ha, ha, ha
Ha ha ha ha ha.

Like I'm so flattered
To be your fourth runner-up
'kay, maybe a little.

We're very sorry
But can't use your submission
We wish you good luck.

FORM RESPONSES TO YOUR FORM REJECTION LETTERS

Who says you can't create a form letter response of your own?

THE GUILT INVOKER

Dear _____,

Thank you for your timely response to the work I submitted several years ago. After looking up _prosaic_ [fill in your editor's own words where underlined] and _insensate_ in the dictionary, I wept. I began to think about my artistic career and realized you were right; I was living a _prosaic_ life, a shallow existence that would never rise above the mire. On several occasions I had yelled at my neighbor, thinking him an _insensate_ fool for repeatedly blocking my driveway with his SUV. Why, I began to ask myself, did I bother to get out of bed each morning and bike to my _prosaic_ job? Even the new curtains I had chosen for the bathroom: _prosaic_.

On Thursday, my beloved cat of eighteen years was run over by my neighbor's SUV. The mangled creature, bleeding in my arms, sent me spiraling into an _insensate_ state, and like a homicidal zombie I approached my neighbor, but then decided, because of your generous insight, not to act on those feelings.

The consequence, of course, has been turning

my *insensate* feelings inward, which is making me unbearably despondent. My art was the one vehicle I had in this world to process the horror that was my childhood. Now, with a dead cat in my freezer and a loaded gun to my head, I ask you . . . were your adjectives carefully chosen?

Regretfully,

_____ (your recently rejected artist)

TO THE BASTARD WHO REJECTED ME

Dear Bastard,

There you sit, poor, poor bastard, buried under towering sloppy piles of narcissistic drivel. The suicide rate in mail-processing careers is high—they say you dream repeatedly of drowning and suffocation.

The Dalai Lama tells me to replace my resentment with compassion, so I have compared your plight to that of a document stamper at the DMV. I visualize your rotten days, surrounded by the scribblings of people whom you think too stupid to live. I imagine the pasty film of coffee on the rim of your chipped Christmas mug and the great work of art you will never have the courage to create yourself. And because I so pity you, I can't muster up the bitterness necessary to close one eye . . . take aim for your heart . . . and pull the trigger as your rejection letter so accurately did.

But, despite the Dalai Lama, I wish you the worst, you Bastard. I can only hope that some day karma yanks the stamp of approval out of your hand and shoves it up your ass.

With deepest sincerity,

_____ (your recently rejected artist)

THE THEN AND NOW

Dear Neophyte,

The highly prestigious _____ Magazine has accepted the piece you so enthusiastically rejected. _____ Magazine would like to paraphrase sections of your rejection letter in an upcoming profile about me. The piece will be your typical "then and now" sort of thing, juxtaposing decades of artistic anonymity with my recent groundswell of success.

Out of respect for your bumfuck organization, _____ is requesting your preference in the matter of your own anonymity. Your options are as follows:

1. _____ Magazine can paraphrase your letter without mention of your name.

2. _____ Magazine can paraphrase with mention of your name. (Imagine your name in the pages of _____ Magazine!)

3. _____ Magazine would consider the inclusion of an "after" quote, for example: "I could kick myself," or "Was I blind?" or something along these lines.

Do let us know at your earliest convenience.

Smugly yours,

_____ (the one who got away)

CPR FOR THE WOUNDED EGO

Some rejections hurt more than others, and a few can even burn for years. The higher your hopes before rejection strikes, the greater the damage. The contest you entered sends you a note to let you know you're a finalist. You call all your friends and say, "Get ready to throw me a party." You may even make it from the top twenty to the final three, the cream of the crop. "It's in the bag," you tell your mother. When you come in second, it's the biggest bummer of all. "Screw my party," you tell your friends. All you can think about is the kudos number one is about to receive. Here you are, once again, part of the moping *unchosen.* You might want to try the following four suggestions before calling Mom yet again in tears.

REVISUALIZE YOUR BEST DELUSION OF GRANDEUR: A GUIDED MEDITATION

Close your eyes, breathe deeply, and conjure up your big moment in the sun. You may want to upgrade or tweak it a bit; maybe your Oprah or Letterman fantasies are

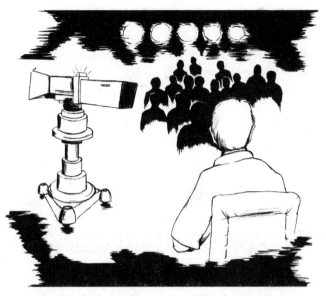

getting stale. Or it could be your delusion needs a complete overhaul—throw in an awards ceremony, a jealous
ex-partner, or maybe that bitch from high school. Refine
every detail, beginning with the atmospherics—the pre-
cise lighting, weather, and potential background music.
You will undoubtedly be thinner and much better looking
in your delusion of grandeur. What outfit best flatters the
new and improved you? Rehearse the script: "Who would
have known that an idea doodled on a napkin could turn
into . . . well, all this!"

MAKE AN ULTIMATUM

If things get *this* bad then I will absolutely bail. For example:
The next time a director bangs his head on the table *during*
my audition, I will take that insurance job with Uncle Phillip.

CALL YOUR FRIENDS AND FISH SHAMELESSLY FOR COMPLIMENTS

Say things like, "Why didn't you tell me I was a talentless shlump?" and "Who was I kidding?" If you get silence on the other end of the phone, then by all means, call Mom.

BUY SOMETHING STUPID

Not just a little stupid, but really, really stupid. For example: a large accordion that you're sure you can teach yourself to play.

WALLOWING: CHOOSE YOUR METHOD

You've been hit hard; don't jump back on that horse too soon. You may need to wallow before mustering on. To each their own method, but here are some paths to guide you through the muck.

BIOENERGETICS, PSYCHODRAMA, AND PRIMAL SCREAM THERAPY

Grab a partner by the chin and scream over and over, "I am not invisible!" in order to watch your spittle build up on his or her cheeks. Or hit your partner repeatedly with a foam bat because *this is your deadbeat agent*. Few things are more healing than strapping on a long cushion and getting the wind knocked out of you by a room full of other cushioned wimps.

TWELVE-STEP MEETINGS

You can find a twelve-step meeting for everything. They've got meetings out there for sexaholics and gamblers; for overeaters and emotional cripples. If you have Fear of Success, there's a meeting just for you. And if you can't qualify for one of these categories, then go for Art Anonymous, which is the exact polar opposite of the Fear of Success meeting taking place down the hall. Here you can sit with others of your ilk and learn phrases such as: "My disease is doing push-ups in the next room." In this forum, you can complain for up to twenty minutes at a time to an entire room full of people—for free. Compare this to complaining one-on-one with a yawning therapist who charges $120 per fifty-minute hour or to your partner, who is *sick to death, no really, really sick to death* of hearing it.

DRUGS AND ALCOHOL

This solution works well for about two hours, until you start puking, or think you can fly. You may feel omni-potent between the fourth and fifth drink, but later, when you're pole dancing with the hot water pipe, you may real-ize omnipotence doesn't protect your inner thighs from scorching.

THE ALTERNATIVE ROUTE

These days, whenever you're down there's always a Reiki student around who's just dying to practice on your sorry charkas. The great thing about New Age practitioners is that they always leave you feeling hopeful. Your channels will be unblocked, you moons aligned, your solar plexus jumping. Go ahead, you say, stick needles in my back, and please light them on fire. How can you *not* feel better when the needles finally come out?

THE HUMILIATION HALL OF FAME

While Andy Warhol once said that everyone would be famous for fifteen minutes, he failed to mention the humiliation that often follows. Sometimes that limelight you're basking in is actually Officer McFadden's halogen flashlight. Artistic disgrace, like poverty, is too often unavoidable. The famous artist lives in the no-man's-land between hero and out-and-out public nuisance. Here are some big names who experienced at least fifteen minutes of fame and shame.

1. Caught by police with his pants down in a rented BMW, Hugh Grant didn't get his money's worth from prostitute Devine Brown.

2. Meg Ryan, dubbed "Trout Lips" by London's *Daily Mail*, not only showed up at the Toronto Film Festival with allegedly some of the scariest collagen enhancements of all time, but her film *In the Cut* was considered one of the worst movies of 2003.

3. Edgar Allen Poe once filed for bankruptcy but was refused because he couldn't pay the fee.

4. Salvador Dali, as usual trying too hard to shock the world, once dressed up in a diving suit to give a lecture. A few problems developed, though—the metal helmet was soundproof, so when he began to suffocate inside it, no one could hear his cries for help. The audience

thought that Dali flailing his arms around was just *Dali as usual*—so they laughed even harder.

5. Paul Reubens (aka Pee-wee Herman) attained tabloid infamy when he was caught masturbating in a Sarasota, Florida, theater. Describing it as "mortifying," he sadly said, "People are laughing at me. . . . I mean I'm just sensitive."[1]

6. Stravinsky, desperate for money, wrote a polka for a performance that featured fifty elephants dressed up in tutus.

7. Mozart wrote a letter begging for a loan, which sold centuries later for one hundred times the amount he was pleading for.

8. When someone once robbed Picasso's garret, they took everything *but* his art.

9. In Cher's biography, *The First Time*, she referred to her 1991 hair care infomercial as, "How to destroy your life in one easy lesson." This faux pas dubbed Cher "Queen of the Endless Infomercial." How Cher recovered remains the most haunting unsolved mystery of the nineties.

10. When Orson Welles made *Citizen Kane*—often considered one of the best films of all time—at age twenty-four, friends urged him to quit then and there because he'd never be able to top it. But the film made little money and many enemies. He once said of his career that he "started at the bottom and worked his way down." In later life, the obese Orson (confined to a wheelchair) would do anything to raise money for his films. Not only was he the pitchman for Paul Masson wines, but he also narrated the theatrical classic *Bugs Bunny Superstar.*

DIC-LIT
If you're a dictator, you don't need to worry about rejection.

• When Saddam Hussein's torrid romance novel, *The Impregnable Fortress*, was selling poorly, he instructed his son, Udai, to order 250,000 copies. "His writing was the literary equivalent to those lurid fantasy murals he had painted all over his palaces," said Jojo Moyles of the Romance Novelists' Association.[3] Although she might just be jealous of his sales.

• Muammar Qaddafi published a book titled *Escape to Hell and Other Stories*. In a review for *Entertainment Weekly*, Alan Smithee wrote, "May we suggest a stint at Tripoli's Writers' Workshop to brush up on, say, plot, character, dialogue, tone, and coherence? Qaddafi often ignores these in favor of the rant."[4]

• Mussolini wrote a bodice ripper called *The Cardinal's Mistress*, with such soul-stirring lines as: "Ah, you do not listen to me, shameless courtesan, harlot. Well, I shall come to get you in this same castle. I shall let the common brutes of the marketplace satiate their idle lusts on your sinful body."[5]

WHAT, ME SELF-PUBLISH?

So, rejected by every publishing house that you've ever heard of? And all the ones you haven't? It might be time to self-publish. There's a reason vanity publishers get a bad rep—there's an inexhaustible number of narcissists who want to see their sappy memoirs, pornographic ditties, and experimental poetry in print. But it's also true that there's a fine history of greats who got their start doing things *their* way. Self-publish a work of genius and the audience will follow . . . and if they don't, your extended family and distant friends will receive a gift-wrapped case of books instead of their annual Wisconsin cheese sampler.

• Walt Whitman self-published *Leaves of Grass* and then wrote a glowing review under a nom de plume. He declared himself "an American bard at last."[2]

• e. e. cummings self-published *No Thanks* with money from his mother. On the half-title page he listed all fourteen publishers that had rejected the book.

• Other famous self-publishers, cutting out the middleman, include Margaret Atwood, Paul Lawrence Dunbar, John Grisham, L. Ron Hubbard, Deepak

Chopra, Dave Eggers, Louise L. Hay, Hugh Hefner, Ernest Hemingway, Nathaniel Hawthorne, James Joyce, Benjamin Franklin, Pat Conroy.

MORE FAMOUS SERIAL KILLER ARTISTS

Some believe that Hitler would have remained atrocity-free if only the Vienna Academy of Fine Arts had not rejected him. Twice. A surprising number of serial killers were, in fact, frustrated artists. This is a caveat worth passing on verbatim to anyone who rejects you. For fun, leave a menacing message on their answering machine that concludes with a deranged cackle. You may want to cite some of the following examples:

• John Wayne Gacy, before he was arrested for the murders of thirty-four children, would often dress up like a clown and entertain the kids at the local hospital. Gacy's amateurish oil paintings of clowns couldn't be given away when he was a free man. Now, post-execution, his paintings go for thousands. Both director John Waters and actor Johnny Depp are proud collectors of Gacy's work.[6]

• Rick Staton, an art dealer and funeral director, has started a company called Grindhouse Graphics, which not only represents the artwork of serial killers like John Wayne Gacy, but also stages "Death Row Art Shows." Among his clients are Charles Manson, who makes stuffed animals out of old socks; Richard "Night Stalker" Ramirez, who makes creepy ballpoint doodles similar to the Pentecostal star he had tattooed on his palm; and Elmer Wayne Henley, who likes to paint koalas. As devoted as he is to promoting the work of these serial killers, Staton concedes that they possess no artistic talent—with two exceptions. Lawrence Bittaker, who murdered, then mutilated, five teenage girls, creates some truly original pop-up greeting cards, and William Heirens, the notorious Lipstick Killer, paints intricate watercolors.[7]

THE LAST-RESORT VENUE

Once rejected by all respectable venues, the artist has no choice but to scrape the bottom of the exposure barrel.

GIVE ME YOUR WALLS . . . PLEASE?

Picasso put up his first exhibit in the back room of an umbrella store. Okay, he was thirteen at the time, but still hardly an illustrious start. Visual artists regularly suffer the humiliation of stepping on restaurant tables with a hammer in their belt loops and nails in their mouth to put up their own "little shows." Often, café patrons may look up askance from their laptops to tell the artist, "Dude, you dropped a nail in my fucking latte." The already hassled manager doesn't want the red sticky dots you've brought her to mark the pieces that sell. "Trust me, we won't be needing these," she is likely to admonish before rudely answering her cell. Worst of all, the artist feels compelled to create a statement to accompany the "little show," which entails linking words such as "departure" and "juxtaposition" in the same sentence. We suspect no one ever *reads* these statements anyway, and to test this theory, we offer the following all-purpose form statement.

Form Artist Statement

When I created this body of work for the _____, it was because no other reputable establishment would have me. I was very careful not to block the exit signs or the enormous promotional banners that co-opt ___ percent of the existing wall space. I have decided not to price these works, because no amount of money could ever compensate for the humiliation I felt when the manager told me to just hold on to my sheet of little red circles. I would tell you what motivated me to create the art that hangs before you, but the truth is, I don't know or care, and neither do you. Thanks for looking!

THE AUCTION DREGS

Most visual artists have vast quantities of artwork that they have, over time, come to hate taking up precious space in their overpriced studios. So rarely does *anyone* call wanting art, that the artist's first response to an auction invitation is, "Sure, I have something to donate." Once committed, the artist soon realizes this means giving away a masterpiece for free. Do lawyers, physicians, and orthodontists give away their work for free? But then the artist is overcome with altruism when considering the cause this art will support: the faces of the abused greyhounds or the children in the Budapest orphanage. Feeling nobly generous, the artist may offer up the finest piece in the pile of dregs and not only transport it to the Holiday Inn function room holding area, but also buy tickets at $50 a pop to attend the gala. And when no one, absolutely no one, bids on the masterpiece, the artist has every right to hide in the bathroom's last stall until even the waitstaff has gone home.

THANKS FOR COMING, AUNT PEG

She has souvenirs from every venue where the artist presented work. Maybe she bought six pairs of lug-nut earrings at the last craft show or came to that Jitters Café opening, where she purchased one of the body print lithographs that the manager never thought would sell, or showed up with a bunch of church friends to see you play Sheila in the tribal love-rock production of *Hair* down at the community center. She is the only relative (including Mom) who does not experience a medical emergency when invited to opening night. She brings flowers, takes pictures, and acknowledges she's in the presence of artistic genius. Aunt Peg is the equivalent to the Valentine's Day card signed, "Don't worry, honey, there's someone out there for you."

FINDING THE STASH BOX

On occasions that warrant the exchange of material goods, such as Christmas, Hanukkah, birthdays, and weddings, many artists make their own gifts. They do this partly because they despise consumer Hallmark culture, but mostly because they have no money at all. These gifts may fall into several different categories:

• **Unsold craft wares:** At the bottom of many artists' closets you will find liquor boxes filled with their own maverick creations, which they can't believe didn't sell at the Ye Olde Holiday Craft Faire. These may include gum-wrapper tea cozies, safety-pin lampshades, and Ross Perot wall clocks.

• **Selections from the dregs pile:** Not bad enough to throw away, and maybe kind of cool? Anything on newsprint, over- or underexposed photos, ill-stretched canvases, abhorrent semi-abstract images that may or may not be elbows.

• **A piece created especially for you!** These love tokens from your artist friend could include a personal photo manipulated to the point of art, a chemically preserved souvenir of your friendship, or your street numbers sculpted in various media.

Over time, if the relationship with the artist endures, the gift recipient is often forced to create a Stash Box—any receptacle (milk crate, Heineken box) in which unwanted gift art is hidden.

The Stash Box is usually kept in an easily accessible cabinet to ensure quick access should the artist stop by on short notice. The contents of the Stash Box are then quickly displayed throughout the house. Inevitably, though, the day comes when the artist rings the doorbell and there's just no time to redecorate, or the worn-out recipient just stops giving a shit what the artist thinks.

When stumbling upon a Stash Box of gifts you've given, see it as an opportunity to reflect on years of artistic development, your own retrospective of sorts. You may want to say something to your friend or relative like, "It's okay, I know you're totally into Target and Pottery Barn and, like, I'm cool with that."

HOW TO FEIGN HAPPINESS AT THE SUCCESS OF YOUR BRETHREN

One of the few things that consoles the undiscovered is knowing that your friends are equally undiscovered. Hopefully, they're even more unknown than you. Therefore, nothing is worse than having to act happy when one of your comrades scores big. Suddenly you are three times the loser you were yesterday. But try to see it this way: Your friend's success could someday provide you with the big contact that either makes or breaks your own career. So don't do anything cruel or petty that you may later regret. For example, don't say, "Well, my God, if you can make it, I guess anyone can!" or "I guess you fucked the big kahuna?" Instead, fake happiness, even though you want to punch their face in. Acceptable responses include:

• Leaving a well-rehearsed message on the answering machine. While you can say "I hate you" in jest, be certain your friend understands how deep your love is, even though you have to be out of town for the opening.

• Sending a bereavement card to the loser your friend used to be.

• Being honest. Say, in person, that you're so jealous you could spit and will have to cease contact until you can see straight. The friend who's on top of the world won't be brought down by your pathetic resentment. In fact, it may add to the glory. Hating you back would be unnecessarily cruel.

CHAPTER TWO

THE TRUTH ABOUT CRITIQUES

Desperate for praise and hungry for intellectual soul mates, the artist naively ventures off to the group critique, also known as the workshop, the tutorial, the feedback session, the third degree, or simply, the crucifixion.

Inexorably, some deflation of the artistic bubble occurs. The extent depends less on the quality of the art than the order in which that art is critiqued. The "critiq-ee" up first is in a position of great advantage and likely to receive the largest proportion of glowing reviews. The reason is simple: The "critiq-ers," your artistic peers, have everything to lose. The nicer they are to you, the more likely you are to be nice to them when their ass is in the hot seat. But as the critique moves on, resentments take root and the group climate becomes increasingly hostile. Pity the poor bastard up last.

Throughout the standard critique, the artist is condemned to silence—unable to utter even the tiniest bit of artistic explanation to justify his work, such as "The painting is upside down" or "The missing twin was kidnapped in Chapter Three." All the artist can do is scrawl notes into his or her notebook and nod approvingly.

This crumpled-up page, and thousands like it, can be picked out of art school trash cans anywhere. In this psychological Vietnam, where anything can happen, the only ally you can hope for is the teacher, who, after all, is *paid* for his or her opinion.

Read those faculty biographies carefully, because trusting your instructor depends on his or her degree of critical acclaim. Ideally, the students should consider themselves lowly in comparison to the teacher, whose pronouncements are THE FINAL WORD. Approval from such a teacher elicits instant group respect and negates all previous nitpicking. But if your instructor lacks the necessary credentials, his or her judgment is only as good as that of the bum sitting next to you. Here we have the potential for a class mutiny. "Just who the fuck are you?" the disgruntled students may rightly wonder.

ARTISTIC EDUCATION

Exactly how qualified are your teachers, and are you, in fact, smarter than they are? There are numerous opportunities for artistic instruction out there—from sonnets with the poet laureate to basket weaving for the incarcerated. Here are the six most common institutions offering artistic education. While state prisons and Harvard University have little in common, they both pay teachers for putting up with you. Here's what to expect.

RESIDENCES AND CONFERENCES

Includes art camps and "working vacations." Here the distance between you and your teacher can be vast, because the faculty lineup reads like a Who's Who of the art world's elite. Maybe you, too, are part of this "other" world because you were chosen to participate on the merit of submitted work. But most likely, you sent in a fat check along with your application and that's why you're here. At many conferences, the role of the student is commonly distorted into that of a fan or even a stalker. Therefore, maintain a safe distance and beware of your teacher's bodyguards.

Teacher answers to: Your Majesty and Please, Come Back.

IVY LEAGUE AND GRADUATE EDUCATION

Here exists what might be called a comfortable distance. The comfort is guaranteed because the student has spent more for tuition per year than he/she is likely to earn for the duration of his/her life. These may be the last years the artist will ever eat regular meals, sleep in heated rooms, or enjoy unlimited access to antidepressants and birth control via the health center. Because professors know this, they are often complicit in maintaining a kind of artificial reality for their artistic students. They are frequently empathetic and likely to buy rounds for the gang at the campus pub. It is not uncommon to read a faculty bio and learn that your teacher, before writing his huge bestseller, was a recreational herbalist and lion tamer. Your teacher's amputated forearm and lack of formal education are big assets here. At the pub, you will soon learn to shut up, drink up, and never interrupt.

Teacher answers to: S'up Doc, O Tenured One, Grand Pooh-bah.

LOW-END HIGHER EDUCATION

Includes state, junior, and community colleges. Distance is minimal but the teacher here is armed with real credits and a grade book that often renders his/her credentials insignificant. The Low-End teacher is often overworked and underpaid and has little interest in being your friend. For justifiable or unforgivable reasons, these facilitators often believe that you, the student, are the leftover crumbs of natural selection, whereas the real talent was picked clean by the Ivy Leagues.

Teacher answers to: The Pardoner, Grade Book Annie, General Patton Sir.

ADULT EDUCATION

Includes all public high schools after sunset and satellite centers for nonaccredited education. Here the distance between teacher and student is negligible. Often the faculty bios in the back of the catalog include such credits as publication in the *Warthog Review* or directorial debuts in Unitarian nativity pageants. And because adult education is a mating hotbed, your facilitator may even double as a matchmaker or potential partner. If the class babes or eligible hunks consistently receive glowing reviews from your facilitator, foreplay may be the dynamic at play.

Teacher answers to: The Hornytoad, Rent-a-Yentl, Hotstuff.

CLINICAL

Includes mental institutions, hospitals, rehabs, and prisons. In these settings the student is most often referred to as the patient, inmate, or simply by their room/cell number. Because participation in the artistic exercise and subsequent critique is often involuntary, it is common for students in clinical situations to inflict physical harm upon their facilitator. It is not uncommon for these teachers to use instructional aids such as the bulletproof vest, the helmet, or the failproof tranquilizer dart gun.

Teacher answers to: Yo Teacher Lady/Dude, Nurse Ratchet, Scumbag.

PUBLIC EDUCATION

Includes elementary, junior high, and secondary schools. Same as above.

WHO'S IN YOUR CRITIQUE?

Each critique has its own group dynamic, and no two are ever exactly the same. The only thing you know for sure is that the poor bastard sitting next to you is every bit as vulnerable as you are. This competitive atmosphere becomes a breeding ground for any number of social phenomena. Just as every shipwreck gives birth to a Gilligan, a Professor, and a Mary Ann, each critique inevitably creates the following profiles. So who are your critique-mates, and who are *you* to them?

LITTLE MISS SUNSHINE (AKA PROZAC PATTY, THE BROWN NOSER, CLASS DRONE)

• Outstanding physical characteristic: good posture

• Constructive comment: "This piece spoke to me of the existential serenity of a baby in the womb."

- Destructive comment: "In this piece I heard the laughter of children."

- Artistic dilemma: How come no one else bakes cookies for the class?

THE SHARE PIG (AKA BLABBERMOUTH, THE MUSER, THE VERBAL TORNADO)

- Outstanding physical characteristic: lips sealed via safety pins (just kidding!)

- Constructive comment: "I was sort of thinking blah, blah, blah . . . (breathe) but then I realized blah, blah, blah . . . but then again blah, blah, blah . . . until I began to wonder . . ."

- Destructive comment: indistinguishable from above

- Artistic dilemma: Why don't I ever get invited to the Mochaccino Barn?

MR. ASININE SUGGESTION (AKA PEA BRAIN, MR. PASSIVE-AGGRESSIVE, THE SPACE COOKIE)

- Outstanding physical characteristic: various body mutations often inflicted by others

- Constructive comment: "Have you ever considered changing the narrator from a twentieth-century feminist lawyer to a fourteenth-century cloistered nun?"

• Destructive comment: "Maybe it's just me—but I thought the narrator was a fourteenth-century cloistered nun."

• Artistic dilemma: Should I write a screenplay about a fourteenth-century cloistered nun?

THE PRIMADONNA (AKA THE WIENER, YOUR HIGHNESS, THE GASPER)

• Outstanding physical characteristics: personal back pillow, irritated contacts, medicated cough drops

• Constructive comment: "Can someone please close the windows in here?"

• Destructive comment: "So this is not a rough draft? Is that what you're telling us?"

• Artistic dilemma: Why does the share pig always sit in the squeaky chair?

WISE OLD SAGE (AKA BEEN THERE DONE THAT, CASANOVA, THE PROWLER)

• Outstanding physical characteristics: tattoos from Nam, indoor sun-glasses, possible comb-over

• Constructive comment: "I used to be just like you, kid. . . ."

• Destructive comment: "I used to be just like you, kid. . . ."

• Artistic dilemma: What the hell is a Mochaccino Barn?

THE ESOTERIC MUTE (AKA THE LONER, BLACK CLOUD, THE SILENT SCORN)

• Outstanding physical characteristics: excessive ink and holes, bleeding cuticles, shredded lips, possible military garb

• Constructive comment: "Can I go to the toilet?"

• Destructive comment: "Your piece? It sucked."

• Artistic dilemma: How many bags of fertilizer would it take to blow up the Mochaccino Barn?

In the Workshop After I Read My Poem Aloud
by Don Colburn

All at once everyone in the room says
nothing. They continue doing this and I begin to know
it is not because they are dumb. Finally

the guy from the Bay Area who wears his chapbook
on his sleeve says he likes the poem a lot
but can't really say why and silence

starts all over until someone says she only has
a couple of teeny suggestions such as taking out
the first three stanzas along with

all modifiers except "slippery" and "delicious"
in the remaining four lines. A guy who
hasn't said a word in three days says

he too likes the poem but wonders why
it was written and since I don't know either
and don't even know if I should

I'm grateful there's a rule
I can't say anything now. Somebody
I think it's the shrink from Seattle

says the emotion is not earned and I wonder
when is it ever. The woman on my left
who just had a prose poem in Green Thumbs and Geoducks

says the opening stanza is unbelievable
and vindication comes for a sweet moment
until I realize she means unbelievable.

But I have my defenders too and the MFA from Iowa
the one who thinks the you is an I
and the they a we and the then a now

wants to praise the way the essential nihilism
of the poem's occasion serves to undermine
the formality of its diction. Just like your comment

I say to myself. Another admires the zenlike polarity
of the final image despite the mildly bathetic
symbolism of sheep droppings and he loves how

the three clichés in the penultimate stanza
are rescued by the brazen self-exploiting risk.
The teacher asks what about the last line

and the guy with the chapbook volunteers it suits
the poem's unambitious purpose though he has to admit
it could have been worded somewhat differently.

(Appeared in the *Iowa Review*, volume 19, number 2, 1989,
pp.169–170)

PASSIVE-AGGRESSIVE STRATEGIES TO GET EVEN

1. When filling out class evaluation forms, ask your facilitator if "ineffectual" is spelled with one "f" or two.

2. Ask the Wise Old Sage about World War I.

3. Raise your hand whenever anyone else begins to speak.

ON BECOMING REVIEWABLE

After toiling far too long in anonymity, you finally get the break you've been waiting for. Perhaps it's a genuine coup and the network casting director calls to say you're exactly the type of person needed to play the zany neighbor; here's Steven Bochco's home phone, he really wants to chat with you. Or perhaps it's not the epitome you dreamed about, but it's a start—*The Warthog Review* wants to publish your sonnet, or you landed the role of Ishmaelite No. 3 in the Hickory Players' production of *Joseph and the Amazing Technicolor Dreamcoat*. No matter how big or small, it's the break you've been after. Fame and fortune can't be far behind. In preparation, you:

- practice signing your autograph

- hire a professional photographer to take your overexposed headshots

- get a TripTik for your multi-city tour

- perfect your deep-waisted bow

- practice saying, "I'm the same person I always was."

- buy frames for your upcoming great reviews

THE REVIEW

You've done it. People are finally taking notice. But with the added spotlight comes the new reality of reviews. And unlike the class critique, which by its very nature is a contained experience, the critic's review tells the whole world whether you succeeded or failed. The fact that it's just one person's perspective is utterly lost on the artist. Indeed, the artist-critic relationship is of the Mommy Dearest brand, with the artist longing for the critic's fickle love. The critic holds all power; the artist can only pray on bended knee that it is wielded benevolently. Once a review comes out, the artist is often too afraid to read it and therefore hands it to a friend. "Did they like it?" the artist asks before the friend has even glanced at the title. Nibbling fingernails, the artist studies the friend's face for clues. What does it mean that he's massaging his temples? He's furrowing, isn't he furrowing?

If the friend pronounces it a good review, the artist is stupefied, then becomes suspicious. "No, really?" And then turns annoying. "How good? Super-good or just so-so good?" The artist then grabs the review and pores over it word by word, half-giggling and half-crying with relief.

A bad review is like a public flogging, worse actually, depending on the publication. The larger the distribution, the greater the damage done. Worried friends rally round. They bring over homemade soup. They dim the lights and talk in soothing tones. One suggests a ceremonial burning of the review. Another discreetly removes all Valium from your medicine cabinet, as yet another confiscates all cutlery, even the vegetable peeler. Even the dog looks worried as he curls up on your feet. Unfortunately, the wider world tends to be less sympathetic.

Here's what kind of response you can expect if you get panned in one of the following venues:

• **Your hometown paper:** Your parents call and tactfully avoid all mention of the review. How's the weather over there? Have you talked to your grandmother recently? Then Mom begins to quietly weep.

• *Sleepy Petals Quarterly Literary Magazine*: A handwritten letter from their editor/critic/marketing director apologizing for what he said about you and asking if maybe you'd like to subscribe.

• *Arts and Crafts Monthly*: Your Aunt Edith, who hasn't contacted you in twelve years, suddenly sends you a sweater and a frowning clown sympathy card.

- ***New York Review of Books:*** Nothing—no one actually reads it.

- ***New York Times:*** Drunken late-night chat-room rants from other artists about how they were also trashed, but in their cases, they didn't deserve it.

- ***New York Times Book Review:*** More than a million people read it. Either pack it in or take a long vacation far, far away from New York.

- ***Variety:*** Tony Danza invites you to be on his talk show anyway. At least your name appeared in *Variety*. When you agree, he bursts into tears because someone, anyone, has agreed.

Statistics show that the pain an artist feels from a bad review is eight hundred times greater than the pleasure they experience from a good one. Or in other words, an artist needs to receive eight hundred glowing reviews (or a Pulitzer/Nobel/Tony/Golden Globe/Emmy) to counteract the sting delivered by a single snark. Furthermore, the average artist dwells on the bad review for far longer than any non-artist friend could ever imagine. Alone in a shuttered room, the artist reads through the bad review so many times, passages become permanently ingrained. Soon the artist compulsively spits out quotes at inopportune moments ("I'd like a Big Mac and a Diet *lightweight intellectualism camouflaging itself as* Coke"). When a friend comes over sniffling about her impending divorce, the artist looks at the sad friend, blinks, and says, "I'm so sorry. But can I just ask you something—do you think I'm a lightweight intellectual?" This is when it turns dangerous. The artist starts to believe the review and sees all failings suddenly writ large. "I am," the artist thinks, "a lightweight. Just plain dumb. Dumber than dumb. I'm a big old dope."

FIGHT! FIGHT!: ARTIST-CRITIC BRAWLS

Profoundly wounded by the bad review, the artist may give up entirely and become an embittered high school teacher who never gives out As. Or the artist may channel that fury into a full-fledged critic rumble. Sometimes it's a war of words, sometimes it comes to actual blows. At one end of the spectrum are classical musicians, who never choose to go mano a mano because of their precious hands. A violinist who soaks, moistens, and manicures every single night would no more consider clenching those darlings into fists than Queen Elizabeth II would send her little corgis into the ring with a pit bull. At the other extreme are the members of bands whose names include "bleed," "screw," "piss," or "wank." Hungover the next morning, they don't know if they bruised their knuckles in the mosh pit or pummeling that bastard from *Creem* magazine. You may, however, respond to the critic in the same way you did to the high school bully. He laughed at the backpack you covered with hundreds of googly eyes and you went off behind a bush to cry.

Eventually you picked up your backpack, jiggled it around, and reaffirmed its coolness. Then you thought of ways to get even. Here are some suggestions for getting back at your critic.

USE CERAMIC ANIMALS

In 2003 the critic Philip Hensher wrote a scathing review in the *Independent* newspaper about an exhibit staged by Tracey Emin, a young Brit Art star. In this review, Hensher asserted that he didn't think it was possible for anyone as stupid as Emin to be a good conceptual artist and that whatever interesting concepts her work included were hit upon by chance. Soon after, this critic started receiving odd items in the mail, including incontinence pads and china figurines of Peter Rabbit. "Someone, clearly, was deliberately persecuting me with rabbits in knickerbockers," he said. In an interview in the *Observer*, he speculated that these items may have been sent by Emin. The artist responded to this accusation by saying, "It's pervy because he's been thinking about me, and imagining that I'm thinking about him. He's imagining me stalking him, and stalking me in turn through the media."[1] Whether or not Emin sent those bunnies doesn't matter. It would freak out most critics if they opened their mail and on the fifteenth day of every month there was yet another ceramic raccoon or panda bear. This is the slow kind of torture you can mercilessly inflict for years, since those little ceramic animals come free with Red Rose Tea.

BUY YOUR OWN AD

On January 26, 2005, Patrick Goldstein published a
review in the *Los Angeles Times* attacking movie studios
for producing shlocky sequels like *Deuce Bigalow:
European Gigolo*. This enraged the star, Rob Schneider,
who then took out a full-page ad in the *Hollywood Reporter*
in which he wrote of Goldstein that most of the world had
no idea who he was and that he probably hadn't won a
Pulitzer because they hadn't invented a category "for 'Best
Third-Rate, Unfunny Pompous Reporter.'"[2]

CONDEMN YOUR CRITIC TO THE UNDERWORLD

In 405 BC Aristophanes wrote a play, *Frogs*, imagining a contest between two dead writers, Aeschylus
and Euripides. In it each man acts as a critic, point-
ing out the others' weaknesses. Aeschylus scores big
with the dis: "You, you jabber-compiler, you dead-beat
poet,/you rag-stitcher-together." Both of the poet-
critics then approach a scale and utter a line from
their own work to see which is weightier. The verbose
Aeschylus beats out his rival and is allowed to return
to the world of the living, while Euripides must stay in
the underworld, which is where most of us feel our
critics belong.

POINT OUT CRITIC'S STUPIDITY

The critic Philip Hamerton wrote various reviews of the paintings by James Whistler. In 1867 he complained that the
artist's *Symphony in White, No. 3* was "not precisely a

symphony in white" since yellow, brown, blue, red, and green were also used. Whistler's annoyed reply was to ask if Hamerton believed "that a symphony in F contains no other note, but shall be a continued repetition of F, F, F? . . . Fool!"[3]

RESORT TO PHYSICAL VIOLENCE

Johann Sebastian Bach called one of his own music students a "nanny-goat bassoonist," meaning someone who makes the bassoon sound like a goat. In response, the outraged student physically attacked him. Bach drew a knife in self-defense, though the fight was broken up before anyone got seriously hurt.

MADAME TUSSAUD'S REVENGE

Artists Darren Phizacklea and Rory Macbeth created a life-size wax sculpture of London's notoriously snarky art critic, Brian Sewell, for an exhibit. The statue peers at a gallery wall, studying a plaque that reads "Waxwork of a Brian Sewell Lookalike, 2000." In his hand he clutches a program from the show in which he's featured.

CRITIC TYPES

Just as music is often classified into rock, jazz, hip-hop, and so on, critics can also be categorized by their particular style and tone.

PHD CRITIC

This critic is primarily a reviewer of poetry and literary fiction. Having spent way too much time in the ivory tower,

"Doc" writes reviews filled with so many Latinate words that even after a dictionary translation, you still have no idea what it means. The good news is that you can pick out any of his phrases at random ("this work is part of the hermeneutic devaluing of the postmodern dictum") and use them as back cover blurbs—you'll sound smart and no one else can define "hermeneutic."

Bribe with: *Oxford English Dictionary*
Hero: Thomas Pynchon

GONZO CRITIC

Found trolling after rock bands, often mistaken for groupie. Tendency to play air drums. Whatever the artist does, Gonzo is right there snorting, sniffing, and screwing along. Is frequently overheard saying to editor, "But dude, I just wanted the band to open up to me." Gonzo's dangerous, because loyalty to band buddies is usurped by need to pay for broken hotel television, rehab, strip club tab.

Bribe with: bail money
Favorite possession: Lou Reed's bar towel

WARM FUZZY CRITIC

This is everyone's favorite critic. Loving and generous as your kindergarten teacher, Fuzzy refuses on principle to review art that doesn't appeal. Why criticize when you can praise? Why tear down when so many need building up? If you hear you're getting a review from Fuzzy, rejoice—it's sure to be glowing.

Bribe with: No need . . . although jelly beans are always appreciated.

Hobby: Collecting Smurfs

BRITISH CRITIC

This critic originally hails from across "the pond" and as such has never subscribed to the American habit of super-sizing. Brit crit believes that the adjective "fine" should be understood to mean exactly what it does, a lesson Brit crit learned way back when at Eton boarding school. When Brit crit got an A, the don said that the work was "fine." The don did not say it had been "the most groundbreakingly earth-shatteringly monumental event to rock modern civilization and a feel-good hit all wrapped up into one sleek and sexy package."

Bribe with: Fortnum & Mason Earl Grey tea (loose, not in bags)

Secret crush: the Queen Mum

THE BIG HEAD CRITIC

These critics are so well-known they have to go to performances incognito. Whatever Big Head says is law. If Big Head loves you, you're set for life. If Big Head hates you, you're sunk for at least five years.

Bribe with: wigs and money

Vacations at: Dan Aykroyd's house on Nantucket

CANNIBAL CRITIC

Sometimes an artist decides to take up the poisoned pen by becoming a critic as well. The artist-critic can be the most vicious critic of all. In much the way that guppies will devour each other in a fish tank, one artist will sometimes attack another out of an instinctual fear that there's simply not enough room for everyone. For example, Evelyn Waugh wrote of Stephen Spender: "To see him fumbling with our rich and delicate language, is to experience all the horror of seeing a Sèvres vase in the hands of a chimpanzee."[4] Equally biting was Truman Capote's assessment of Jack Kerouac's *On the Road*: "That's not writing, that's typing."[5]

Bribe with: Promise that when it's your turn to review *their* work, you'll be nice

Favorite movie: *Silence of the Lambs*

GIMMICK CRITIC

This critic loves rating systems. Fingers up or fingers down. The circles are empty, a quarter-full, half-full, three-quarters full, or, whoa boy, all the way full! Gimmick Critic reviews a lot of art and wants to make sure that there's variety in the ratings. Even if everything was fantastic, too many full circles on a page looks like a Pac-Man run amok, and so Gimmick will inexplicably give a half-circle to something deserving a full. Too many empty circles—also not good, so Gimmick will be forced to give bad art a full circle. The trick, therefore, is to make sure your art gets reviewed on a day when there's already a disproportionate number of less-than-fulls.

Bribe with: Phases of the moon poster

Dreams of: Roger Ebert naked and covered in whipped cream

OPERATIC CRITIC

This critic may or may not do opera reviews—the name comes from the critic's screeching sensibilities. A piece of art is either so delicious it causes drooling puddles of delight, or else it is pointless flotsam drifting on a river of sewage waste. "Figaro" has no sense of objectivity and undergoes massive emotional swings. When reviewing a work, Figaro has been known to openly weep, burst into hic-cuping guffaws, blanch with horror, then fall sound asleep.

Bribe with: monogrammed hankies

Favorite descriptors: "heartbreaking," "dazzling," "putrid"

A FRIEND'S GUIDE TO HELPING YOU THROUGH A PARTICULARLY BAD REVIEW

Cut out this helpful handout and distribute it to your friends so they will always know how to support you after a bad critique.

• **Help the artist grow thicker skin:** Offer critiques unrelated to your friend's precious work. For example, hairstyle, pet training, cooking ability, tiki collection. Describe the new paper lantern hanging over the artist's bed as "garish Japanese clashing with the otherwise turn-of-the-century shabbiness." The artist's new orange futon cover? Definitely thumbs down. That favorite pair of bowling shoes with smiley-face laces? Thirty degrees on the hundred-degree hipster scale. After a few days of this, the artist is inured to pain.

• **Gird the artist's loins:** An artist waiting for a review is a whimpering bag of nerves. Wrap your friend in a fleece blanket, snuggle, and coo. This will calm the artist and create a bond of trust and love between the two of you, which you will need later when you reassure your friend that the reviewer was a big fat idiot.

• **Point out that taste is a relative thing:** Ask the artist to make a list entitled "The Ten Grossest Foods." Then take the artist on a scavenger hunt through the neighborhood trying to find people who have these foods in their cupboards. Once you've found someone with a jar of black jelly beans, have a little talk with the artist about how the things that one person loathes are delicious to another.

• **Hold a believe-a-thon:** The tender artist ego is routinely attacked by waves of self-doubt that only multiply after a critique. To counteract this, get a video camera and tape all the artist's friends saying, "I believe in you. I know you will succeed." Remind friends that the artist will be scrutinizing the tape for any signs of mockery or wavering; therefore, friends should be instructed not to laugh.

• **Play anagrams:** Take the bad review and rearrange letters as best you can so that instead of having, "A lackluster showing," you now have a license-plate-style affirmation: "Go shock! R U a stellar win!"

• **Cut and Paste:** Remove the disparaging words to turn your friend's bad review into a glowing one. According to Dave Simpson, a critic for

London's *Guardian* newspaper, a performer named Valentine Flyguy had publicity fliers made up that used this quote from a *Guardian* review: "The audience fell about and cheered." However, what that review originally said was: "Flyguy made jokes about black Americans. The audience—young, drunk and all white—whistled and fell about." Similarly, Simpson recalled how in 1999, another *Guardian* critic said that a film "could be wonderful . . . unfortunately it isn't." Within hours a publicist shortened the review into a blurb that read—you guessed it—"Wonderful (the *Guardian*)."[6] Example: You don't need to flog yourself. Music this outrageously monotonous should be declared an illegal substance—consumption may cause boredom so lethal that you'll drop to your knees with hands clenched and beg for something more. Cut-and-Paste Review: With music this outrageous, you don't need a monotonous illegal substance. You'll drop to your knees with hands clenched and beg for more.

TOP TEN SLAM

The following pontificators gain entry into the Curmudgeonly Critic Hall of Fame for their ability to sit in scornful (and often amusing) judgment of others. Our wish to you, Artist, is that you never get a review that rivals these.

• Australian art critic Robert Hughes said of Francis Bacon: "Some art is wallpaper. Bacon's is flypaper."[7]

• In 2003 novelist and bully critic Dale Peck published a review of Rick Moody's memoir, *The Black Veil*, that began: "Rick Moody is the worst writer of his generation."[8]

• In the *New York Times Book Review*, Elizabeth Judd wrote of Pam Houston's novel *Sight Hound*: "It's pointless to sharpen your [critic's] pencil too energetically over silliness of this magnitude."[9]

• Dorothy Parker famously responded to Mussolini's book by saying: "This is not a novel to be tossed aside lightly. It should be thrown with great force."[10]

• In 1889 the editor of the *San Francisco Examiner*, having published one article by Rudyard Kipling, declined to accept any more of the author's work. The reason? Not knowing how to use the English language. "This isn't a kindergarten for amateur writers."[11]

• London's *Financial Times* reviewed the play *Enigmatic Variations* in which Donald Sutherland starred, describing the play as "stupid" and sleep-inducing and Sutherland as "an awkward stage animal, with his muzzy consonants and his ill-tuned, foggily projected voice." As if this weren't bad enough, the critic for the *Independent on Sunday* wrote: "'Enigmatic Variations' is built round twists. I wouldn't want to give anything away—least of all tickets."[12]

• Rumor has it that Samuel Johnson once told an aspiring writer that his manuscript was both good and original. Alas, there was a catch: "What is good is not original," Johnson declared, "and what is original is not good."[13]

• In a review of the movie *Catwoman* published on the Web site rottentomatoes.com, critic John Beifuss wrote: "A stinky hairball on the soiled rug of the summer blockbuster schedule, gruesome enough to have been ejected from the esophagus of Bill the Cat . . ."[14]

• Urban Cinefile Critics said that the movie *Alexander the Great*, was "a garbled, over-stuffed turkey force fed with historical events until its liver explodes in a spectacularly colourful and violent bloodbath."[15]

• Responding to Ben Affleck's holiday picture *Surviving Christmas* Craig Roush of Kinnopio's Movie Reviews wrote: "A movie you watch with a half-cringe on your face, waiting to see the lengths to which Affleck will humiliate himself."[16]

CREATE YOUR OWN REVIEW

Fill in the blanks. This is actually how many of the pros do it.

The new work by _____ is reminiscent of
NAME OF AN ARTIST
_____ _____ . It causes the intellect to _____
ADJECTIVE   TYPE OF SNACK FOOD   VERB
and the heart to feel _____ . The best aspect of
ADJECTIVE
this work is its use of ____ and _____
COLOR   TIME PERIOD
atmospherics. It's challenging _____ may
STATE OF EMOTION
come from the Bohemian lifestyle that _____
NAME OF ARTIST
engaged in, including _____ parties and late-
ADJECTIVE
night _____ sessions with _____ . While
VERB   CELEBRITY NAME
such experiences can open the mind to _____
ADJECTIVE
ideas and _____ experiences, it can also
ADJECTIVE
cause _____ . _____ is clearly poised
TYPE OF DISEASE   NAME OF ARTIST
on a cusp and will either push through the _____
NOUN
and break new ground, or else ____ backward
VERB
into _____ irrelevance.
ADJECTIVE

CHAPTER THREE

DAY JOBS

In *Man and Superman,* **George Bernard Shaw** wrote, "The true artist will let his wife starve, his children go barefoot, his mother drudge for his living at seventy, sooner than work at anything but his art."[1] But sometimes an artist's elderly mother is not as industrious as the artist might hope, and thus he or she is unable to pay the rent. At this point, the artist may be forced to punch in the old time card. Yes, your job may suck, but do not overlook the perks. Too often artists pass right over fabulous employment opportunities simply because they don't understand what these jobs can do for *them.* For this reason, we offer a list of part-time jobs an artist might consider when Mom isn't pulling her financial weight.

SHOW ME THE MONEY

THE TEMP

Okay, there's not a whole lot of artistic inspiration to be gained by joining the cubicle captives, but you do get access to copy machines and unlimited free coffee, and no one expects you to know what the hell you're doing. The artist temp is often seen as a sexy interloper, although rarely at first. In the beginning the full-time office drudges will snicker behind your back at your freakish hair, the tattoo your black turtleneck can't hide, and the inscrutable bumper stickers over your bowling bag. In a few days, however, curiosity will get the better of your office mates. "Who is this temp?" they will start to wonder. As an artist, you will be seen as a representative of a mysterious and distant culture, and just like all such representatives afforded a certain amount of enticing eroticism. Use your first paycheck to stock up on birth control—you're going to be busy.

Justification: I'm gathering material.
Humiliation Quotient: "You're an artist. Can you make a DO NOT JAM THE COPIER sign?"
Perks: "Free" office supplies

THE WAITER

This is the quintessential artist job. In a recent Employment America survey, 94 percent of all artists had waited tables. What can we say about waiting tables that you don't already know? Except this: Denny's uniforms will melt if you cook them in the microwave.

Justification: In 1986 Francis Ford Coppola sat in section eight.
Humiliation Quotient: Singing "Happy Birthday" to Francis Ford Coppola
Perks: "Free" grub

TEACHING

The artist may turn to teaching after working on one too many Chuck E. Cheese birthday parties. You get real health insurance benefits, summers

> **Justification:** Spreading the joy
> **Humiliation Quotient:** Spitballs
> **Perks:** Summer

off, and, if you're lucky, multidenominational holidays like Kwanzaa and Rosh Hashanoh. It all comes down to classroom management and the tranquilizer dart gun you keep in your desk drawer.

STRIPPER

If on camera Kathy Bates and Dennis Franz can bare it all, you can do it too for a few bucks. This is the time to claim your inner exhibitionist, to let go and try out those moves you perfected while dancing in front of your bedroom mirror to the artist formerly known as Prince. A little-known fact: Four of the girls who regularly appear humping a pole in the Bada Bing Club scenes on *The*

> **Justification:** My body is my art.
> **Humiliation Quotient:** Greasing the pole before the curtain goes up
> **Perks:** Ye olde silicone tax write-off

Sopranos went to Juilliard. Just keep telling yourself, "It's a springboard."

THE CLOWN

Do not underestimate the power of the clown. People love clowns (except for the 80 percent who want to beat them up and the 20 percent who do). Clown suits demand almost as much attention as the naked body, but when you're a clown, you get to be someone else and take on a persona. Find one that best reflects your worldview:

Weepy Clown? Prozac Clown? Sarcastically Bitter Sicko Clown? Karen Reinholt, aka Peppermint the Clown, charges one hundred dollars to enterain kids with a magic show, balloon animals, and a puppet show. Sound like a perfect job? She warns that in the past anyone who put on a funny wig and big shoes was considered a clown, but that now "we're getting rid of that myth because we are getting highly skilled and trained clowns regardless of their dress. We're showing that clowning is professional entertainment."[2] To help you become one of those highly skilled professional clowns, we're passing along a primer on making a balloon animal sure to delights the kiddies. You're on your own for the magic and the puppets.

Justification: The love, the tears
Humiliation Quotient: Your Gremlin breaks down en route to Joshua's birthday party.
Perks: Makeup conceals identity.

BASIC BALLOON WIENER DOG

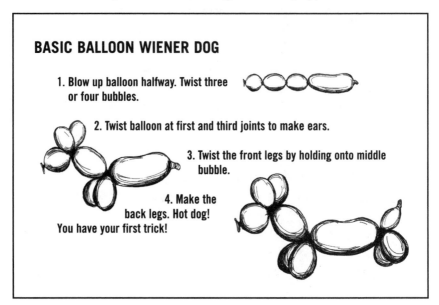

1. Blow up balloon halfway. Twist three or four bubbles.

2. Twist balloon at first and third joints to make ears.

3. Twist the front legs by holding onto middle bubble.

4. Make the back legs. Hot dog! You have your first trick!

NUDE MODEL

For the youthful model, this is the ultimate narcissistic power trip. You are the center of attention, your armpit hair is scrutinized and transformed into visual poetry—you are Venus, you are Apollo, you are the Madonna, you are Adonis hurling his discus. At least this is what you tell yourself as your arms cramp up and Wanda at easel number six accuses you of shifting your elbow *again*. Meanwhile, Frederick at easel number four can no longer see your left nipple.

> **Justification:** Free art school
> **Humiliation Quotient:** "Yes, one is bigger than the other."
> **Perks:** Expose self legally

AND FOR THE SENIOR NUDE MODEL

> **Justification:** Supplement Medicaid
> **Humiliation Quotient:** "Mr. Shrinky"
> **Perks:** You don't have to get up from your wheelchair.

What, you don't need time to just sit, unencumbered, and ponder? Here's an arena where wrinkles, bunions, and varicose veins trump the easy-to-draw butter-smooth skin of youth. You're a challenge, so cash in on those liver spots.

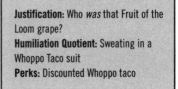

LIVE ADVERTISING

You might be dressed like a tube of Pepsodent or a can of Pringles, but don't worry—no one can see your face. If you pretend you're off-off-off-off Broadway, being tooth-paste can seem downright

> **Justification:** Who *was* that Fruit of the Loom grape?
> **Humiliation Quotient:** Sweating in a Whoppo Taco suit
> **Perks:** Discounted Whoppo taco

avant-garde. You're not simply giving out coupons, you're a postmodern prop, an existential declaration.

Caution! Temperatures inside inflatable costumes can reach up to 150 degrees, causing suffocation and heat stroke. Make sure your costume is equipped with a battery-operated fan and a professional cold vest.

TELEMARKETER

No one loves a telemarketer—you're despised, a thorn in everyone's side, but isn't that what Dada was all about? Be controversial. Push society's buttons. And here's a little-known fact: *The Jerry Springer Show* gives free tickets to telemarketers because they are so likely to snap. Who knows what TV exec might be on a treadmill watching you hurl a chair at that cross-dressing, two-timing, seventy-nine-year-old trash-talking ho?

Justification: You try to find a job with a steer horn through your nose.
Humiliation Quotient: Even Mom hangs up on you.
Perks: Calling your friends in Prague

SUBWAY BUSKING

The first step to successful busking is garnering pity. Get a lame dog or train one to limp. Steal a wheelchair from the hospital curb drop-off. The subway's got great acoustics, but it's not your only option. Consider all places where people exit with their souls crushed—the downtrodden need a good dose of your shamelessly pandering joy. Busk in front of the DMV,

Justification: One hundred rolls of pennies and you got fifty bucks.
Humiliation Quotient: The train pulls in during you're a cappella crescendo.
Perks: Good acoustics

funeral parlors, the courthouse, nursing homes. (May we suggest "Stairway to Heaven"?)

Justification: Retire at thirty.
Humiliation Quotient: At Dylan concert, your Lexus gets egged.
Perks: 401(k), etc.

CORPORATE SELLOUT

You're rich and your artist friends don't like you anymore. Neither do we.

THE CREATIVE RÉSUMÉ

While the manager at the Mochaccino Barn was greatly impressed by the way you filled in your job application, particularly your nifty gel pen and the endearing habit of dotting your *i*'s with tiny eyeballs, it's time to start shooting higher. Put away that gel pen and get ready to write a real résumé. Don't despair, think "creative nonfiction." Your résumé can be a work of art. It has to be—you have no marketable skills. There's a fine line between lying outright and presenting yourself in the best possible light. Below is an example of the uninspired all-too-honest résumé. Following that is the same résumé doctored up to land you that job that you're totally unqualified for.

Artist's Actual Résumé (Pre-Tweak)

EDUCATION

- **Grassy Meadows Preparatory School.** Expelled in tenth grade after meth lab discovered in locker
- **Woodrow Wilson High School.** Belonged to no clubs, slept with photography teacher, voted Most Likely to Be Executed, suspended for burning American flag in school trash can. Proudest accomplishment: spray painting "Bourgeois Pigs" on second-floor bathroom mirror
- **Nutley State College.** Graduated SIMS major (Studio for Interrelated Media Studies). Final thesis title: Innocence Corrupted—while wearing only a diaper, the artist spent three weeks quarantined in storefront window folding origami devils out of dollar bills. This display not only incited devil haters to prostrate themselves in prayer, but was also used to exemplify abuse of the national student loan program. The *Nutley Observer* said: "This art is a stunning example that de-evolution *is* taking place right here in New Jersey."

WORK HISTORY

- **Head Barista Bitch.** Mochaccino Barn, Nutley, New Jersey
  — Responsibilities: Extricating smelly vagrants, blending grande cappuccino mocha crèmes, cleaning bathroom, working cash register
- **Movie Extra.** Played Despondent Teen #16 in *American Pie 2* and fetched creamers for Jason Biggs
- **Nude Model.** Senior Citizen Adult Ed Life Drawing class
  — Responsibilities: Sat on cold metal chair holding fly swatter and sunflower at the Golden Oaks Alzheimer's Center
- **Subway Busker.** Played clarinet on corner of Seventh Avenue and 54th Street
- **Live Advertisement.** Wore inflatable Pringles can and handed out free samples and coupons

Artist's Tweaked Résumé

EDUCATION
- **Grassy Meadows Preparatory School.** Head of applied chemistry club
- **Woodrow Wilson High School.** Mounted numerous photography events; President, Eleventh Grade Chapter of Anti-Defamation League; school beautification committee
- **The Nutley College of Art and Design**, BA Media Studies. Final thesis titled "Manipulation of Japanese Papyrus as an Exploration of Western Capitalism." The *Nutley Observer* described the exhibit as "A stunning example of art right here in New Jersey."

WORK HISTORY
- **Retail Process Associate**, Mochaccino Barn, New Jersey
  — Responsibilities: Community relations, Italian-English translation, hygiene specialist, fiduciary expert
- **Featured in American Pie 2** and **Dietary Consultant** to Jason Biggs
- **Entertainment Coordinator**, Golden Oaks Geriatric Center
- **Principal Clarinetist.** Performed regularly at Carnegie Hall
- **Executive Sales Purveyor**, Proctor & Gamble
  — Responsibilities: Field researcher, promotion strategist

Remember to cover your bases: Bribe your references or give Mom an alias (she always was a great actress). A stunning recommendation may deter a thorough background check.

BUMMER DAY JOB MATCH-UP

Before they hit the big time, even the famous had to shovel some shit. Here are some famous shit shovelers and the shit they shoveled. Match the star to the shitty job:

Rod Stewart	department-store Santa
Ellen DeGeneres	coffin maker
Rock Hudson	slaughterhouse lackey
Christo	kennel cleaner
Burt Lancaster	sexy avocado pusher
Ozzy Osborne	hooker
Michael Douglas	exterminator
Billie Holiday	corpse beautician
Whoopi Goldberg	hairdresser
Cyndi Lauper	pineapple chunker
Sean Connery	gas pumper
Madonna	car washer
Dustin Hoffman	coat checker
Warren Beatty	doorknob maker
Courteney Cox	oyster shucker
Angie Dickinson	Tampax hawker
Danny DeVito	grave digger
Kevin Nealon	vacuum cleaner salesman
Bette Midler	roach powder salesman
Luke Perry	lingerie salesman
E. B. White	janitor

Answers:

Rod Stewart was a grave digger.

Whoopi Goldberg was a corpse beautician.

Warren Beatty was an exterminator.

Angie Dickinson promoted avocadoes, aka "the green love food."

Billie Holiday was a hooker.

Dustin Hoffman was a janitor.

Ellen DeGeneres was an oyster shucker.

Danny DeVito was a hairdresser.

Courteney Cox was a spokesperson for Tampax.

Kevin Nealon was a department-store Santa.

Rock Hudson was a vacuum cleaner salesman.

Christo was a car washer in a garage.

Cyndi Lauper was a dog kennel cleaner.

Burt Lancaster was a lingerie salesman.

E. B. White was a roach powder salesman.

Sean Connery was a coffin maker.

Bette Midler was a factory pineapple chunker.

Ozzy Osborne was a slaughterhouse lackey.

Luke Perry was a doorknob maker.

Michael Douglas was a gas pumper.

Madonna was a coat check girl.

ART SLOB REDUX

So you have an interview with the Man. Or maybe at your temp job, Peg from personnel has told you that casual

Friday doesn't mean fishnets and go-go boots, especially for guys. It's time for an art slob redux.

STRIP THE HARDWARE

All you punks and metalheads, you're likely to be ten pounds lighter without your dog collars, nose rings, and wrist-to-elbow bangle sets. So let's liberate the safety pins from whatever flesh they're fastened in—you can use them to hold up the zipper of your vintage plaid trousers.

MASK YOUR MUTATIONS

Flesh-colored stage wax works fairly well to putty in those stretched-out piercings. Two coats of the cheapest cover stick, plus some dusting powder will turn that tattoo into a mere hematoma on your neck—just remember, *don't sweat*. A herringbone scarf draped flatteringly over those fuchsia dreds will make you look like a cancer patient, thus avoiding further inquiries from Peg. For guys, you might need to sigh maudlin asides about pernicious anemia due to those extensive chemo treatments in order to justify the bowler hat you won't take off.

J. CREW FAKE-OUTS

Surrender two outfits, then mix, match, cut, staple, glue, and voilà! You've got a week's worth of unhip corporate-wear.

FOR WOMEN

Sacrificial Outfit Number One

taffeta prom dress with cigarette burns

chenille bed jacket

vinyl cha-cha boots

thrift shop clarinet case

1. Remove puffy dress sleeves, tulle petticoats, and enormous rhinestone orb from bodice. Cut bottom third to make knee-length. Staple hem. Glue excess material to temper plunging neckline and patch cigarette holes. Use leftovers for headband, belt, and neck scarf.

2. Saw down cha-cha spike heels to acceptable three inches. Remove homemade pom-poms from zippers. Spray paint from bubblegum pink to black.

3. Peel off stickers (Hydrahead, Pee-wee's Playhouse, Oingo Boingo, etc.) from clarinet case and complete the attaché with press-on gold initials.

Sacrificial Outfit Number Two

vintage Brentwood frock

pinstripe bolero jacket

bowling shoes

Wonder Woman lunchbox

1. Cinch frock at waist with excess prom dress taffeta.

2. Shoe-polish bowling shoes from two-tone to a conservative monotone.

3. Accessorize bolero lapel with enormous rhinestone orb (à la Bulgari brooch).

4. Don't worry, you don't have to spray paint your Wonder Woman lunchbox; simply camouflage it in a small D'Agostino's bag.

MAKEOVER BASICS—WOMEN

First of all, remove all black nail polish. Like most art girls, you have one pair of shitty hole-riddled stockings that are far beyond the magic of nail polish repair. Therefore, why bother with stockings at all? Why not dab a tiny bit of red nail polish on your bare knee and ankle? This will create the illusion of pantyhose. Spray cheap perfume to mask stench of nicotine and booze.

Use masking tape to de-fur. And you probably don't own an iron, so hang the dress outside a hot shower for ten to fifteen minutes to steam out any wrinkles.

Monday
Sacrificial outfit number one

Tuesday
Sacrificial outfit number two

Wednesday
Taffeta dress, bolero jacket, taffeta scarf, bowling shoes, and clarinet attaché

Thursday
Brentwood frock uncinched, taffeta headband, bed jacket, modified cha-chas, D'Agostino's bag

Friday
Turn Brentwood frock inside-out, bunch chest fabric and pin at center with orb. This creates the fashionable bow-tie effect and hides the obvious seams and darts. Directly under the breast line, cinch with taffeta belt to create a not-so-naughty baby-doll look. It's dress-down Friday, so you won't need a camouflage jacket. Don't make the mistake, however, of thinking you can wear your canvas high-tops or de-bag your lunch box.

FOR MEN

Sacrificial Outfit Number One

> leisure suit

> vintage Hawaiian shirt

> antique golf shoes

> clip-on tie

1. **Use electric sander to grind away golf cleats and remove fringe flap.**

2. **While your white or baby blue leisure suit might pass muster at the Rotary Club, it probably won't slip by Peg, despite your metrosexual defense strategy. Polyester is notoriously hard to dye, so use three packages of navy Rit instead of one.**

Sacrificial Outfit Number Two

> mod plaid pants

> concert T-shirt

> smoking jacket

> scuff-toed rockabillies

1. Turn the concert T-shirt inside out.

2. Duane Reade sells iron-on patches for $1.99. We know you don't have an iron, so glue patches onto smoking jacket elbows and give yourself an academic flair.

3. Polish those rockabillies.

MAKEOVER BASICS—MEN

First of all, buzz cut your hair, because Peg wants to see Opie, not Sid, in the mail room. Also your burns, soul patch, and Fu Manchu have got to go. Your vintage clothes probably smell like cigars and mothballs. This destinkification recipe works every time: Fill your bathtub with water. Add a cup of Lysol, one can of tomato juice, a tablespoon of hydrogen peroxide, and one bar of Ivory soap. Stir with crowbar. Submerge clothes overnight. Then hang to dry.

Monday
Sacrificial outfit number one

Tuesday
Sacrificial outfit number two

Wednesday
Leisure suit, inside-out T-shirt, rockabillies

Thursday
Mod pants, Sonic blue shirt, smoking jacket, golf shoes

ARTISTIC GIVEAWAYS

Gnawed-down, burnt-sienna-stained cuticles

Referring to cube mates as "Vulcan drones"

Multiple toe rings with your open-toe mules

Your Karl Marx screen saver

Signing your bathroom graffiti "the anonymous interloper"

Gumby shoelaces

The noose you hung above your desk

Friday

Remove patches from smoking jacket and put on leisure suit. Turn concert T-shirt right side out and don't shave your soul patch—it is, after all, casual Friday

NOT THAT YOU'RE A SLACKER, BUT . . .

So you keep getting subpar job evaluations. Don't let this contribute to your already low self-esteem. See it as further proof that you've got your priorities straight by saving energy for what really matters. While the rest of the world thinks you're a lazy, good-for-nothing, hot-dog-suit-wearing slug, we know different. The work that really matters is the work you don't get paid for. You're only lazy on the clock—slacking *off* the clock is when you need to worry. For comparison's sake:

• Louisa May Alcott wrote as many as fourteen hours a day. She pressed down so hard with her pen that she permanently paralyzed her thumb. "I'll be rich and famous and happy before I die," she said, "you'll see if I won't."[3]

• Charles Dickens regularly got up at seven a.m., took a bath in cold water, then began writing.

- Zora Neale Hurston said, "I shall wrassle me up a future or die trying."[4] Once, while out gathering material for a novel, she had to pass a test to gain the trust of a Creole conjurer by lying naked facedown on a couch for sixty-nine hours without food or water, with a snakeskin touching her navel.

- Diego Rivera painted more than two and a half miles of murals in his lifetime.

- Christo and Jeanne-Claude sold drawings to earn the $21 million to finance their Central Park Gates exhibit. Christo works seventeen hours a day, seven days a week. Jeanne-Claude is more of a slacker, putting in only twelve- to thirteen-hour days.

BRINGIN' HOME THE BACON

George Gershwin not only had big bucks, he also loved his money dearly and had a fourteen-room penthouse on Riverside Drive with a piano even in the gym. Gershwin, however, was an exception—most artists have little money, and if they do, they feel strangely guilty and morally superior to it. Woody Guthrie thought money so corrupted people that he actually gave it away. Chopin declared rather dramatically, "I am a revolutionary, money means nothing to me."[5] Emily Dickinson called her poems "snow," to declare their purity from the monetary world. William Pope.L, conceptual artist, sat on a toilet perched on a ten-foot tower while eating copies of the *Wall Street Journal*.

Some are simply too spaced out to care. Hokusai paid bills

by handing over closed envelopes of money directly from his clients. Sometimes he overpaid, sometimes he underpaid. Similarly, Jean-Michel Basquiat would set wads of money on the counters of art supply stores and let the clerk figure out how much he owed. Diego Rivera left large uncashed checks lying around for years. Salvador Dali never quite got the hang of counting American money. And Mozart's extreme poverty didn't seem to faze him—when the firewood ran out, he grabbed his wife and danced to stay warm.

CASHING IN: GET-RICH-QUICK SCHEMES

So maybe your facial tattoos have made you unhireable, or you just can't stomach working for the Man. You need cash and you need it bad. The following are alternative routes to lining your pockets. Some may require further decay of your moral fiber, but the rent's due and you're down to a single tube of cadmium red.

COUNTERFEITING

You may want to try your hand at forgery, particularly if you work late hours at the Copy Cop. However, trying to pass off your strangely crisp twenties at the local bodega might require a boldness that many artists simply don't possess. Ethical culpability often causes the artist to sweat profusely and break into tears while waiting for change.

CHAIN LETTER

You originate a chain letter, sending it to all your friends. The letter instructs them to add their name and send five dollars to the person at the top of the list (you), and send copies to all their friends. This scheme promises that soon a big pot of money will return to all participants when they're at the top of the list. Be sure to include the heinous accidents that befell all previous nonparticipants, as well as copious references to poverty-stricken geniuses who received more than one million dollars' worth of five-dollar bills in less than one month. All you need to begin is five dollars, an envelope, and the willingness to lose all your friends.

ART AIRPLANE

Each airplane has eight Passengers, four Stewardesses, two Copilots, and one Pilot. Everyone starts out as a Passenger—ticket cost is somewhere between $50 and $500. In order to become a stewardess, a Passenger must recruit eight more Passengers. Stewardesses eventually move up to Copilots, and Copilots eventually move up to be Pilots. At the top of the pyramid, the Pilot supposedly cashes in big. Unfortunately, what usually happens is something like this: Bob, the sculptor, doesn't sell enough seats. Sally, Bob's painter girlfriend, currently a Stewardess, breaks up with Bob because this Airplane shit is just more evidence that Bob lacks any determination whatsoever. Bob jumps ship and takes Jim, the slide guitarist, with him. The next Airplane meeting is highly emotional; several newly recruited Passengers stand up, exclaim "Fuck this shit," and heroically kick open the double metal doors of the Copilot's loft before disappearing, like cowboys, down the dusty stairwell. Before long, the six suckers still on the plane are plotting ways to hurt—really, really, hurt—Bob because he started this whole fucking dissent thing. Meanwhile, Sally has run off with the Pilot.

REAL ESTATE

Shakespeare did this and earned more off his wheeling and dealing than he did from any of his plays. The problem is that pesky downpayment to get in on the game. Now's the time to clean out Aunt Peg's gutters and in general make yourself lovable to all your elderly home owning relatives.

DIE

Occasionally market forces and fate combine so that an artist's worth increases dramatically after death. A rather sicko example of this involves the artists Robert Mapplethorpe and Keith Haring. After Mapplethorpe died on March 9, 1989, of AIDS, Christie's New York auctioned off some of his property for the benefit of Mapplethorpe's newly launched AIDS charitable foundation. The hottest seller was an amphora-style vase decorated by Keith Haring. Just two months before, Haring had announced that he had AIDS during an interview with *Rolling Stone* magazine. Writing for *Artforum*, Judd Tully reported that like "vultures" bidders were already circling Haring.[6] The vase, which Christie's estimated would earn

$8,000 to 10,000, ended up selling for a staggering $231,000. Haring died just a few months later.

MOVE TO AUSTRALIA AND GET A GRANT

Between 1989 and 1996, the Australian government paid $11.5 million to sixty-five financially struggling artists. The fund originated when the then prime minister, Paul Keating, discovered that the country's arguably greatest pianist, Geoffrey Tozer, was scraping by on $9,000 a year teaching piano to Keating's own son among others. Keating set up a program using tax dollars that would give out grants worth between $45,000 and $66,000 a year to needy artists. "They were people at the top of their game but with no means of income," said Keating. "They were people on which our country depends but it gives them no support."[7] If you don't get a grant, however, you're screwed. A recent survey titled "Don't Give Up Your Job" found that one third of Australia's artists live below the poverty line, having a mean "creative income" of $12,230. On the upside, Australia has some really good beaches.

SKIMP ON SUPPLIES: YOUR BODY IS YOUR ART

A Stratocaster's going to set you back a minimum of $700. A single tube of Winsor & Newton cadmium green pale oil paint costs

$20, and even though you need it *right now*, how often will you use it in the future? That Great American Novel you're planning on writing will require a computer, and even if you get one refurbished, you're looking at $500. If the day job you've got isn't allowing you to tuck away the bucks for your art, we'd like to suggest you use your body. It's yours and God knows it's cheap. As you stand naked before the world with your ingrown hairs, puckering cellulite, and freakish toenails exposed, remember this: It's a fine line between soliciting approval and provoking outright hatred. Few things are more satisfying to the general public than pummeling mimes with rotten tomatoes. If you're undeterred, the following are inspirational examples of performance art that won't deplete your bank account.

• Janine Antoni's exhibit "Gnaw" featured the artist gnawing on a *really* big block of lard. (Estimated cost: $40.33 for eighteen tubs of Crisco, $1.67 for dental floss)

• For a piece titled "7 Years of Living Art," Linda Montano wore one color per year for seven years. Imagine the money you'd save on off-color fashion.

• Tehching Hsieh made a splash in New York when he announced that he would spend a full year in a cage he'd set up in his Brooklyn loft. An assistant came in to give him food and dispose of waste, but otherwise the artist lived an extremely ascetic life. He didn't talk, read, write, listen to the radio, or watch TV for a full year. Just think about it, no bills from the cable company and nothing to do but pluck lint out of your navel. (Estimated cost: $35 for extra-large dog cage)

• Vito Acconci spent the period between 1969 and 1973 building up a seminal body of work. During this time he transformed physical space by masturbating in an art gallery. (Estimated cost: free fun!)

• In 1971 Chris Burden made a name for himself by aiming a .22 caliber gun at his arm and firing. The bullet was only supposed to graze his skin's surface, but instead created a hole in his flesh. He later crawled on a floor of broken glass in his underwear, semi-crucified himself to a VW Bug, and had himself bolted to the floor with electrical wires. Next to the wires were buckets of water so close that anyone in the gallery could knock a bucket over, thus electrocuting him. Not surprisingly, his MFA thesis for UC Irvine was called "Five Day Locker Piece." He fasted for five days in preparation, then locked himself in a school locker with one jug of water and another one to piss in. (Estimated cost for all the pieces: $10 for gun from NRA Convention, $4.90 for case of Bud bottles, $1 for crucifixion nails, $2.40 for jugs of water)

• Carolee Schneemann's 1975 piece "Interior Scroll" featured her removing a scroll from her vagina. (Estimated cost: $.58 for small roll of paper usually found on adding machines)

• Ann Hamilton covered a suit of clothes with toothpicks, porcupine style, put it on, and photographed herself. (Estimated cost: $4.75 for case of toothpicks. The outfit you're wearing will do just fine.)

• Andre Serrano had the great idea of using NEA funds to submerge a crucifix in a cup of his own urine. It got U.S. senator and art-hater Jesse Helms really upset, ultimately inspiring him to pass legislation that barred the NEA from funding obscene art. (Estimated cost: NEA pays for $1.35 for urine cup and $12 crucifix. The cost of upsetting Jesse Helms? Priceless.)

At the end of the day, you've scrimped and slaved and quite possibly embarrassed yourself beyond reason for the almighty dollar. So what do you do with that paycheck now? The artist must resist the temptation to order appetizers and full carafes of sangria. What you don't need are more snowglobes and Slinkys; what you do need is to fork over the rent. And if you're freeloading with Mom or long-suffering friends, a contribution of toilet paper, cat food, or generic pasta will buy you some time. After all, it's the least you can do.

ARTISTIC DWELLINGS

While the artist needs less square footage than your average suburban slob, who really wants to live in a refrigerator box? Even a shopping cart festooned with handmade ornaments is still a shopping cart, and potential lovers are sure to flee when they find out your "pad" is in a culvert. Let's face it, you need some place to store your eccentric collectibles, not to mention create your art.

If you're lucky, you're able to take Virginia Woolf's advice and have a room of your own, meaning you live in one place and create in another. Your "work space" exists not in a corner of your ten-foot-by-ten-foot apartment, but in an actual alternative location. Many artists say this is critical for creative health. It also impresses your pals to say you're heading to "your studio." If you live in a city where you've got to spend upward of $500 a month to secure any sort of separate creative space, you tell yourself that paying such an exorbitant amount of money is the best incentive to buckle down and get to work. You may arrive exhausted and uninspired from your day job, but once you remind yourself that the space is costing $17.20 a day, those creative engines start smoking. Or else you move your crap back into the corner between your bed and only closet.

Studio space has always been hard to come by. At the turn of the century, Parisian artists could rent cheap nooks at La Ruche. This round beehive structure had originally been constructed as the wine rotunda for the Great Exposition of 1900. Rent was thirty-seven francs a quarter—dirt cheap, but then there was also no gas, electricity, or running water. The building was an oven in the summer, an igloo in the winter, and the rats didn't care what season it was. No artist, though, was ever evicted—for nonpayment of rent or anything else. It's easy to see why artists like Soutine, Kisling, Chagall, Modigliani, and Brancusi had no complaints. If you can find a space like the ones at La Ruche, rent it right away.

The fact is, you're most likely not going to have that eight-sided sun-filled writing space enjoyed by Mark Twain, nor E. B. White's quaint little boathouse, nor Calder's black barn, nor Warhol's silver Factory. But maybe whatever crappy little space you're working in today will be the stuff your honorary museum is made of. Or, should you toil in absolute obscurity, you'll at least be able to afford your own modest fishing shack.

Even the seemingly romantic French utopia of van Gogh's cottage in Arles—a place with an amiable village postman, naturally distressed furniture, lively peasants, and fields of glowing sunflowers—had its drawbacks. Van Gogh's buddy, Paul Gauguin, described Arles as "the dirtiest hole in the south." The main reason van Gogh lived in his Yellow House (as it was known, for its yellow wash) was because it was cheap compared to apartments in Paris. While he did enjoy the rural life, van Gogh was also tormented by the crows and mosquitoes that attacked him as he painted outdoors.

Despite its drawbacks, van Gogh thought the Yellow House had great potential and invited many artists to come establish an art colony there. Only one actually did: Gauguin. Some say that by the time Gauguin showed up, van Gogh was already suffering bouts of impotence due to both syphilis and excessive absinthe abuse. The men's rivalry over art and virility culminated one night in a heated argument during which van Gogh supposedly chased Gauguin down an alley with the razor that he later turned on his own ear. That evening, when Gauguin returned to the famed Yellow House, he found a trail of blood leading up the stairs. Van Gogh was passed out and nearly dead. "Wake this man with great care," Gauguin told the policeman. "If he asks for me tell him I have left for Paris. The sight of me might prove fatal."[1] After this incident, van Gogh and his Yellow House became increasingly unpopular with the villagers. Eventually they organized a petition and had him banished from his beloved Yellow House altogether.

THE TEN MOST DEPRESSING OR ROMANTIC ARTISTIC DWELLINGS

Take heart: Other artists have met with mixed success. From crumbling hovels to sun-splashed country estates, artists have run the real-estate gamut. Where you hang your hat is likely to fall somewhere within the following spectrum:

1. **GAUGUIN'S HOUSE OF PAIN: AFTER TAHITI,** Gauguin headed to the Marquesas Islands hoping to find the master craftsmen and naked cannibals that Herman Melville had written about. Instead he encountered a vanishing native culture and a nasty Catholic mission church. Undaunted, Gauguin built what he called his "House of Pleasure," seduced yet another fourteen-year-old native girl, and began hosting a number of all-night parties. The local priest worked himself up into a froth and began vilifying Gauguin in his Sunday sermons. Soon attendance at the House of Pleasure dwindled to nil and the Party Animal found himself sentenced to three months' imprisonment for various offenses against the community. While awaiting his appeal and suffering from syphilis and hepatitis, the painter holed himself up in his studio, where he consumed large quantities of absinthe and morphine. After days of heart palpitations, coughing blood, and finally delirium, Gauguin died alone in his famous House of Pleasure.

2. **MARY CASSATT'S CHATEAU DE BEAUFRESNE, "HOUSE OF THE BEAUTIFUL ASH TREE":** It was here, in her redbrick country home, that Cassatt painted her peasant children by day and frolicked with Degas and Manet into the wee hours of the night.

3. **ERIK SATIE'S DUST PIT:** For twenty-seven years, Satie did not allow a single visitor to enter the small room he rented above a noisy café.

The neighborhood was said to be so dangerous that he carried a hammer with him for protection. Upon his death, the dust was found to be so thick that the curtains and furniture had begun to deteriorate.

4. **GEORGIA O'KEEFFE'S RANCHO DE LA BURROS:** In 1934 O'Keeffe began renting a New Mexican ranch house as a summer residence. One spring she showed up for an unscheduled visit and was furious to find people in "her" house. When its owner, Arthur Pack, pointed out that she didn't own it, she demanded that he sell it to her. He agreed, but the grouchy O'Keeffe still wasn't satisfied. "I wanted enough land for a horse," she grumbled, "all Arthur would sell me was enough for my sewer!"[2] In her paintings O'Keeffe captured the dramatic views surrounding the ranch and used the flat-topped Pedernal mountain so often that she called it her "private mountain."[3]

5. **CHAIM SOUTINE'S SLAUGHTERHOUSE:** This Russian-born expressionist was big into painting meat. In his Paris workshop on the Rue du St. Gothard, he hung an enormous side of beef in his work space. Wanting it to look fresh, Soutine would send his model, Paulette, down to the slaughterhouse to fetch fresh blood. Soon the carcass began to rot and the meat inspectors came knocking. The model begged the inspectors to "be kind, you see, he is painting the beef." The agreeable inspectors fumigated the stinky workshop and injected the carcass with ammonia.

6. **SALVADOR DALI'S FISHING HUTS IN PORT LLIGAT, COSTA BRAVA, SPAIN:** The painter purchased the first hut in 1932, supposedly to distance himself from his tyrannical father. Over subsequent years, he and his wife, Gala, would buy more huts, renovating them into a surrealistic compound, complete with staircases that led nowhere, labyrinths, and giant eggs balancing on the roofs. Although the couple enjoyed entertaining and would dress in outrageous outfits, including eyeball

costumes, they preferred not to have anyone stay overnight; therefore, the compound included no guest rooms.

7. **MICHELANGELO'S ALLEY FLAT:** Though he could afford otherwise, the sculptor spent his last thirty years living in a depressing flat in a small dark alley. His modest dwelling was said to be thick with cobwebs.

8. **ZORA NEALE HURSTON'S HOUSEBOAT:** She called it the Wango. On this dreamy floating hovel, Mrs. Hurston was said to have traveled not only the Halifax and Indian rivers, but a whole 1,500 hundred miles from Florida to New York.

9. **MODIGLIANI'S VAGABOND TRAIL:** After studying art at academies in Florence and Venice, the young Italian painter moved to Paris in 1907 ready to begin a flourishing art career. Within weeks he was penniless, traveling from one flea-ridden flophouse to another. Sometimes he would trade a drawing for a drink. When he couldn't pay the rent, he'd end up back on the streets pushing his belongings in a wheelbarrow. He died impoverished at age thirty-six from TB. The next day his wife, Jeanne, who was also a painter and nine months pregnant, jumped from a window of her parents' home, killing herself and their unborn child. At one time Modigliani had said, "I want to be a tune swept fiddle string that feels the master melody, and snaps. . . ."[4] Indeed, he seemed to get his wish.

10. **VANESSA BELL, CHARLESTON FARM HOUSE:** This Eden in the heart of Sussex Downs is enough to make any artist starving in a two-hundred-square-foot studio (without sunlight) want to vomit. But take heart, it didn't start out that way. In 1932 Vanessa moved with her two children, her partner and fellow painter Duncan Grant, and Duncan's lover, David Garnett, into the damp, chilly, rundown farmhouse, which had been built back in Elizabethan times and looked it. They tore down the

ugly peeling wallpaper and began stenciling the walls with their own designs. They painted gorgeous frescos on the front of the old bathtub and over the fireplace. They transformed their junk-shop furniture with upholstery they made themselves. One of Vanessa's children, Quentin Bell, wrote, "When we arrived [the garden] contained fruit trees and some potatoes and practically nothing else that I can remember apart from what had once been an earth closet."[5] Soon, however, they had turned the space into a gorgeous walled garden with mosaics, statues, willow trees, and even a pond. Here the artists of the Bloomsbury group, including the writers E. M. Forster, Vanessa's sister Virginia Woolf, and Lytton Strachey would drink wine, create art, and ponder the pros and cons of their notorious bisexual love triangles.

CONTEMPORARY HOUSING FORECAST

While housing standards have gone up over time for the general public, not so for artists. Amenities such as plumbing, baseboard heat, double pane windows, and prime cable packages continue to elude those driven to create. Because it's damn hard to find an old cement garage in the middle of the city where the landlord is jiggy with chamber pots and drum fires, the holy grail remains securing a rent-controlled apartment. This elusive quest drives many artists into urban holding patterns that can last up to twenty years. Most end up living with other artists in quarters akin to the hulls of slave ships. Such close conditions can be responsible for massive social turmoil. Remember, two months together in scenic Arles was all it took for van Gogh to start chasing Gauguin around with a razor blade. And *their* house had big windows, separate bedrooms, *and* a working fireplace.

As predictable as the hairs they will leave in the rust-stained sink, here are the common archetypes of roommates with whom artists inevitably are forced to share the bathroom:

THE VULTURE

They float from one bad sublet to the next, befriending the near-dead in any given building in hopes of inheriting that $420-a-month two-bedroom. They will often be spotted banging aggressively on apartment doors with one hand while clutching a bouquet of flowers in the other.

THE DISH GENIE

This is a mysterious mutation of the out-and-out slob, because you never see dish genies actually dirtying dishes. They tend to create large meals late at night while others are sleeping. In the morning, dish genies deny any connection to the sink full of greasy pots and pans. They also hate sharing and label their milk and enormous containers of brown rice with markers.

DEMOLITION GIRL

Watch out for this manic craftsperson because she will steal the slats from under your mattress and create unstable shelving units above the industrial sink. She has been known to chop through plaster walls to expose the nonexistent brick beneath.

THE NONARTIST

These are the ones who have come to study your kind. Often they assume the role of loft-parent, cooking nutritious meals the way Mom used to. In exchange they may pester their roommates to lend them clothing, dye their hair, and sponge paint their bedroom walls.

THE LOFT SIREN

The loft siren doesn't want any other women around. Ideally, she rooms with four to five straight men, all in committed relationships. She tends to fry eggs in provocative lingerie, exit the bathroom in nothing but a hand towel, and drop porn in the DVD player as if by accident.

Don't get attached to your roommates. In America the average citizen relocates six times. For artists that number is twenty-plus, and it's rarely for greener pastures. Real estate agents have a term for artists: Risk Oblivious. "What?" the wide-eyed artist may reply, "you say there's a crack house next door? Do I look like someone who *discriminates* against drug lords?" In the pre-gentrified neighborhood, the artist proudly lives with a finger on the pulse of a dysfunctional culture so resplendent, so exhilarating, that life itself becomes performance art. Outside is the stuff that network dramas are made of and the kind of shit that a kid from the suburbs could only dream about. Sure, you're paying twice the rent of your neighbors, but still, it's cheap. So what if Mom visits with a can of Mace in her patent leather purse?

In this way artists can be compared to indicator species, such as the spotted owl. When they move into a neighborhood, you can bet it will soon be a cultural Mecca. Before long the rents will double and the bulletin board at the new mochaccino bar will be advertising displacement support groups. The terms "realtor extortion" and "scum lord" get volleyed from one wobbly table to the next. The question remains: Are artists to blame for the exploitation that inevitably comes along with them? To this the artist may reply: Can the spotted owl be blamed for chopping down the forest?

A neighborhood's transition might look something like this:

Skeletal frames of vehicles ⟶ SUVs

Stray dogs and crack whores ⟶ Heterosexuals, strollers, golden retrievers

Dealers with beepers ⟶ Cell phone jabber

Garbage can bonfires ⟶ Trees wrapped in white lights

Dominican social club ⟶ Starbucks

Out-of-tune ice-cream truck ⟶ Dog-grooming van

Inevitably, that artistic Eden becomes a self-denying prophecy. The pioneers who settled the territory can no longer afford their rents and, anyhow, they wouldn't be caught dead in the homogenizing soul-sucking Benetton. At this point the artist might begin yet another migratory phase—sacrificing urban hip for something more practical. Before you jump to defeatist conclusions, nonhip dwellings offer a myriad of advantages, from communing with nature to being your community's one and only artist.

The following are assessments of the six dwellings most familiar to the modern artistic community. Your average artist is likely a veteran of them all.

THE URBAN LOFT

If you're lucky enough to have one, it won't be anything like Andy's Factory or the vast luxury inexplicably granted to artsy types in Hollywood movies. Instead, you and your half-dozen roommates are probably living in your raw space illegally, and you claim a mere partitioned corner as your own.

Pros: Mentioning your "loft" at parties, roller-skating to the bathroom, exposed brick, fooling around in the industrial elevator

Cons: No heat on weekends, sharing one hot plate with six people, inhaling the toxic fumes of the first-floor body shop

THE URBAN HOVEL

Comparable to Europe's more exotic-sounding "garret," this retreat is often a fifth-floor walk-up without roof access. Not uncommon to find the bathtub in the kitchen and a shared bathroom in the hallway. Toilet seats may be worn into the shape of an ass.

Pros: See roommates bathing

Cons: See roommates bathing. Harry from 5B brings his crosswords to the toilet.

THE COUNTRY DIGS

You may try to delude yourself with images of O'Keeffe's New Mexico ranch or Thoreau's tiny cottage, but you're most likely here because of the nervous breakdown you had in the city. Also, it's dirt cheap.

Pros: No car alarms, fresh air, *space* to work

Cons: Crickets that sound like car alarms, bored rednecks, employment opportunities limited to Wal-Mart and Piggy Wiggly

YOUR MAMA'S ATTIC

So you've come home again with your tail between your legs. No one understands better than Mom, even though she thinks Christo is an all-vegetable shortening.

Pros: Free rent, free meals, washer and dryer, sympathy, the opportunity to heal the emotional scars from your childhood

Cons: Having sex at own risk, lawn mowing, the opportunity to open the emotional scars from your childhood

SUBURBAN GARAGE

Here's a cement box that doubles as a rehearsal space. You are most likely here because your friend's mom was kind enough to take you in when your own mother kicked you out of the attic.

Pros: Realization of lifelong Partridge Family fantasy

Cons: Mrs. Partridge doesn't live here anymore, SUV exhaust fumes

BOTTOM DWELLERS

Let's say Mom's turned that attic into a sewing room or den, or your frustrated landlord is willing to set up a cot by the furnace until you come up with a rent check— these are likely scenarios that land artists in basements. Occasionally the basement is used as a studio, though the term itself is an oxymoron.

Pros: Furnace is warm

Cons: Slugs, blinding light bulb, sexual activity highly unlikely

THIS OLD NEST

Regardless of its placement, home is the nest, the womb where the artist retreats to drink alone and sob facedown into the garbage-picked mattress. Real estate options are so painfully limited for the artist that decor turns out to have heightened importance. An artist's pad is the only protection from the cold, cruel world outside. It serves as padded cell, cocoon, genie bottle, work space, and uterus all at the same time. With the right decor, the artist can turn any old hole in the wall into a slightly better hole in the wall.

THE TEN COMMANDMENTS OF ARTISTIC DECOR

1. Thou shalt never buy anything from Pottery Barn (okay, maybe one thing if it's on sale).

2. Thou shalt not covet thy neighbor's staple gun.

3. Thou shalt own at least one piece of Elvis memorabilia.

4. Thou shalt not buy brand-new furniture, then fuck it up with a hand sander.

5. Thou shalt not have matching chairs.

6. Thou shalt have parts of, or one entire, mannequin.

7. Thou shalt hang your own artwork, but only in the bathroom.

8. Thou shalt have pet hair on thy old shitty sofa.

9. Thou shalt have at least one string of year-round Christmas lights.

10. Thou shalt have two bodega prayer candles next to thy stash of condoms, unless you're a lesbian, in which case you have them on either side of your Melissa Etheridge poster.

DECORATING STYLES

Your nesting aesthetic depends on your personality, your budget, and your willingness to dig through your neighbor's coffee grinds for that Yogi Bear jelly glass. Some artists go for the bold and dramatic—the fuchsia walls, the moose head beret-hanger. Others prefer their surroundings more intimate—Grandma's afghan, their eleven-year-old spider plant. And some take any damn bread crate they can get their hands on.

SAL'S BOUTIQUE

At the Salvation Army you can often find a velvet couch better than the one on *Friends* for well under $100. You can also buy sixties afghans, Engelbert Humperdinck albums, and prom dresses for your mannequin. Almost always there is an old chain-smoking misanthrope in the back room whom you must report to for prices. It is unwise to try to cut deals with the misanthrope, because he or she can inflate even a marked price at will. "Why?" the misanthrope barks. "Fuck you, don't ask me why."

THE COMPULSIVE YARD SALER

"I'll give you my bicycle plus this leather jacket for that velvet Elvis."

Like gamblers, Compulsive Yard Salers have been known to come home without their shirts. They can turn rabid, exchanging unpleasantries with other yard salers such as "Right, you spotted it first and I'm Saddam Hussein—nice to meet you." They are often seen bouncing off of streetlights as they carry home up to ten large objects at a time.

THE IMPULSIVE GARBAGE PICKER

"Can you believe someone was actually throwing this away?" Impulsive Garbage Pickers come home with such useful items as urine-stained mattresses, broken wheelchairs, dying rubber trees, and cinder blocks. Garbage Pickers are usually on strict rehabilitation programs enforced by their partners and therefore turn shifty eyed when quietly hauling their booty into any number of contraband storage areas (behind the furnace, in the rafters).

GOD BLESS MAMA

This nostalgic and cost-cutting style utilizes all objects saved by your mother throughout the Oedipal stage of your childhood. These objects are often highly functional as well as gender specific, such as your ballerina bedside lamp, your Minnie Mouse alarm clock, or your Luke Skywalker quilt and sheet set.

DOLLAR STORE KITSCH

This eclectic and thrifty style is often religious in nature and, best of all, well under five dollars. In Spanish dollar stores you can readily find holographic Last Suppers and apostle ashtrays, as well as six pairs of tube socks for $4.99.

FORCED MINIMALISM

A bread crate is also a table, is also a bookcase, is also a laundry basket. A Mexican blanket is also a couch cover, is also a curtain, is also a coat. A cinder block is also a doorstop, is also a planter, is also a weapon.

THE *FRIENDS* MYSTIQUE

This style comes straight off the floor of stores like Domain, Shabby Chic, and Anthropologie. The furniture's been hand-sanded by poor Mexicans making eighty cents an hour to give it the weathered look of an authentic antique. You can kid yourself into believing that the piece aged with dignity in the attic of a French farmhouse or admit that it's fake and costs more than most artists make in a month. If this is your style, then you're most likely a trust fund recipient masquerading as an artist. Fact: Artists don't live like the people in *Friends*.

GOYA MADNESS! FIVE GREAT TIPS FOR RESURRECTING YOUR BEAN CANS

Don't throw out your cans. They are the building blocks of affordable style!

1. **Goya shelving unit**

2. **Goya window prop**

3. **Goya leak catcher**

4. **Goya condom holder**

5. **Goya organizer**

RAINY DAY CRAFT PROJECTS FOR THE ARTISTIC DWELLER

The true artist respects the power of recycling. No, this isn't about being "green" or socially responsible—just resourceful. Behold your power to create.

DEAD ROACH AND DUST-BUNNY WREATH

Recycle the contents of your Roach Motels with this spooky, attention-grabbing conversation piece.

You will need:

- eight-inch Styrofoam wreath base

- twelve to eighteen medium to large dead roaches

- twenty-four to thirty-six sewing pins

- twelve to eighteen dust bunnies

- one to six dead centipedes (optional)

- Aqua Net hair spray

With sewing pins, secure roaches and dust bunnies to Styrofoam wreath base. Add optional centipedes if desired. Fix with six generous coats of Aqua Net hair spray.

SARDINE CAN COIN DISPENSER

No more digging under the couch cushions for Laundromat change! With this simple coin dispenser, the silver you need is right at your fingertips.

You will need:

• three large sardine cans

• three nails

• a wall

• spare change

Begin by rolling back the sardine key and nailing the bottom of the cans directly into your hallway wall (don't worry about "finding the beams"). The cans should be facing the tall way, with the key closing upward toward the ceiling and opening downward toward the floor. Fill cans with stacks of change—one with quarters, one with nickels, and one with dimes. Two or three stacks of quarters, or three to four stacks of nickels, or four to five stacks of dimes should fit in most large sardine cans. Once your cans are filled, roll the key back up toward the ceiling to keep your change from falling out. As you spend your change, simply roll the key down to access the shorter stacks. When all the change is gone, refill accordingly.

WINDOW BAR MAKEOVER

Why does crime prevention have to be so unattractive? Here are some simple tips to beautify your jail rails.

You will need:

- nine to twelve bricks (easily found in any crumbling tenement)

- six pint-size cardboard milk cartons

- dirt

- morning glory seeds

- fishing line

- two bottles of Rolling Rock

- two bottles of Boone's Farm red wine

BEFORE

AFTER

Begin by stacking bricks lengthwise between the window bars. You may need to secure them with a few pieces of strategically placed fishing wire. Make six stacks, some tall (up to four bricks high) and some short (one or two bricks high). Keep one brick off to the side. What you want to create is several brick pedestals of various heights. Next, cut the tops off of your milk cartons, fill with dirt, and plant your morning glory seeds. Place the milk cartons on top of your brick pedestals. Now, consume your wine and beer before smashing the bottles under a towel with your spare brick. Pick pieces of colored glass that you find aesthetically compelling and wrap them like presents in fishing wire. The bottle bottoms tend to catch light particularly well. Hang your new sun catchers from the bar across the top of your window. If you do not have an across bar, simply string one piece of fishing wire horizontally across. Step back and admire.

HEY, I'VE GOT A GREAT IDEA!: A BRIEF HISTORY OF THE ART COLONY

Undoubtedly someone in your little group has uttered these words, inspiring fantasies of a rural compound (though not too far from the stimulations of the city) with sun-drenched studios galore, fields of wildflowers, and perhaps even a few horses. Like the Bloomsbury group, you and your artist friends will divide your time between creating lasting works of genius and getting laid. Maybe, but only if you have a friend like Mary Cassatt, whose huge trust fund can finance the whole thing. After all, you don't actually think you could afford anything with a name like Chateau de Beaufresne, do you? But maybe, you say, just maybe we can all *pool* our resources . . . and gosh, it's so zany it just might work.

Here's why your art colony, unfortunately, is likely to fail:

1. The Wal-Mart won't buy your homemade greeting cards.

2. There are ten of you and only two openings at the Piggly Wiggly.

3. Following your dream is not an actual job.

4. The rich kid took off to the Caribbean.

5. Should we pay the mortgage or buy more garden gnomes?

One contemporary artist colony that apparently manages to circumvent these problems is the Zendiks commune. All fifty or so artist members work exclusively on the "farm." They support righteous causes, make art, and don't make anyone sell flowers at the airport. Many of these young hippies are also hotties (check out the Web site). So why shouldn't you quit your job tomorrow and join up? Well, first of all, the commune's in Texas. Yeah, Texas. Second of all, you have to share your ecostructure with many others from your tribe. And third, you may be coerced into "recruiting," which involves the insidious peddling of *Zendik Arts* magazine.

THE EXILES

So you've had it with the feeble-minded, the culturally anemic, and pretty much every other idiot sipping lattes at your local Starbucks. It's time for you to run away from home. You want a grander, more enlightened milieu. Artists have been doing it for centuries. The only difference between this and running away as an eight-year-old with six bucks and a pup tent is . . . well, there's really no difference. Okay, maybe you have eighty bucks and can set up that tent all by yourself.

Where do all the artists go? Wherever all the other artists go: Florence, Paris, Costa del Sol, Prague, all over Mexico—though art Meccas are only authentic art Meccas for so long. Ben

Mallalieu, writing for the *Guardian*, noted that while Montparnasse was once the artistic and literary capital of the world, it has since been absorbed into the rest of Paris. The creative energy that existed there, he claims, is gone not only from Paris, but from society at large. At one time Montparnasse "was a place where you could live and work cheaply, and behave unconventionally, a community of free souls far beyond the pale of respectable society."[6]

Artists who want to create their own contemporary Montparnasse may at first feel discouraged. In cool cities such as Paris, London, and Berlin, real estate is affordable only to doctors, lawyers, CEOs, and "creative" accountants. Even once-viable warehouse districts are now filled with stockbrokers who think riding in an industrial elevator is walkin' on the wild side. We've heard that Vietnam's still got some cheap real estate, but who can afford the airplane ticket to get there? Same goes for Chile, and Mexico's coast has gone too commercial.

Therefore, why not stay local? The key is for the artist to find a place so undesirable, so economically devastated, that at least 50 percent of the residents are on some kind of public assistance. Most often this means long-dead industrial towns where crumbling factories dominate the landscape. Such towns can be identified by their abandoned drive-in movie theaters with rusty pickups still parked at the speakers as if aliens came and sucked out the passengers in 1946. To create your own Montparnasse, find such a town and then begin to circulate rumors to attract others of your kind. The philosophy is simple—if you fake it, they will come. Tell them:

"David Byrne has a summer place out there."

"Jagger showed up once, played 'Angie' at the dive next to the Laundromat."

"I found a Monkees lunch box at the Salvation Army for fifty cents."

"There are only a *few* spaces left that actually face the river."

"The Mochaccino Barn is coming—*and* the Thai restaurant."

This is supposedly how the whole Prague thing started. They said, "Kafka, Velvet Revolution, and real cheap beer," and 30,000 young foreigners infiltrated the city.

"Real cheap beer."

THE UGLY AMERICAN

If you still want to run away from home equipped with a passport, be prepared for the natives to hate you. This is particularly true all over Europe, thanks to George W. and his penchant for invasion. In France you may be confronted by any number of angry mobs. "Yes, certain Americans do call them Freedom Fries," you will sadly admit, "but not *me*." Being an American in Europe is as humiliating as walking around with your mother in her bathrobe and curlers. In pubs, violent locals may ask you to defend foreign policies you know nothing about—thus proving that all American are ignorant pigs. "No," you must tell them, "I don't drive a Hummer or work for Donald Trump. Or been fired by him." If you're feeling particularly defensive (or suicidal), you may want to remind your new friends of the following: European colonialism, the Inquisition, World War II. Though the best way to avoid all conflict may simply be to lie.

TIPS ON ACTING CANADIAN

1. Buy a pair of Roots "Negative Heel" shoes.

2. Iron a maple-leaf patch on your faded denim jacket.

3. Claim to be from Vancouver, home of the radical *Adbusters* magazine.

4. Say "about" like you're saying a-boat.

5. Ask for a Kokanee, then act surprised that the pubmaster doesn't carry Canadian microbrews. Settle for a Moosehead.

THE PARROTHEADS

Contrary to popular belief, Jimmy Buffett did not invent the parrothead movement. Gauguin was out sticking a lime in his coconut before Jimmy Buffett was even born. So were Jack London, Herman Melville, and Robert Louis Stevenson. The allure of the tropics is hard to resist: balmy weather, minimal living expenses, and uninhibited girls who are not only naked but willing to be your wife. That said, many painters still claimed they were there for the "light." Henri Matisse described going to the tropics "to see the night and the dawn light that must have another density." He proclaimed, the Pacific light "is a deep gold tumbler in which one looks."[7]

Should you decide to embark on a tropical journey of your own, beware of the following:

1. To the natives, you = walking dollar sign.

2. Bartering with market women who live in tin shacks *is* the ugly American.

3. That idiot with the salt-shaker necklace? Don't be seen with him.

4. The changing mole on the back of your neck.

5. Rum punch does not make you more creative.

6. It only *looks* like play money.

7. If you're white, braided hair looks stupid.

CHAPTER FIVE

ARTISTIC STYLE

SHORT DUDES, UGLY DUDES, AND SCARY-LOOKING WOMEN

"There is not one female comic who was beautiful as a little girl." —Joan Rivers[1]

People who become artists often share strikingly similar traits with those who become criminals: abusive parents, traumatic childhood events, and marked scarcity of the brain chemical seratonin. In some cases, being good-looking cancels out the above misfortunes, but throw ugly into this already precarious mix and nine times out of ten, you get an artist or a criminal.

Lots of people have dark holes inside them, but some have sewers—places so deep and putrid it's best to keep them covered. Art can be the pipeline that the putrid sewage leaks out of. Most great art, as well as clever con games and multimillion-dollar bank heists, comes out of a guttural hunger for recognition, particularly by those who have spent their lives unnoticed, or worse, known only as freaks. "Love me for my brain," the beauty-challenged tell us, "and keep the lights down low."

FAMOUS BEAKS AND HONKERS

- Hans Christian Andersen

- Marc Chagall

- Miguel de Cervantes, author of *Don Quixote*

- Igor Stravinsky

- Dustin Hoffman

- Barbra Streisand

- Rembrandt

- Marc Twain

- John Updike

- Salman Rushdie

- Adrien Brody

THE HOTTIES

Occasionally, artistic hotties will step in and hog the limelight. These golden ones seem to have everything going for them. For example, artist Matthew Barney's not only hot, but he's also a football star and Yale graduate and is now making a series of hip indie films called the Cremaster series. It's easy to see that there's no level playing field.

Why can't the beautiful remain on soap operas, where they belong? The homely and suffering resent hotties for having an illegitimate advantage no matter how dysfunctional their childhoods might have been. Let the arena where music videos have yet to infiltrate remain untainted by the hotties. The beautiful who sneak in through the back door are tolerated, and a talented hottie like Frieda Kahlo is even celebrated for *not* shaving her unibrow. Here are some other artists we not only admire, but also like to look at:

- The young Truman Capote

- Cindy Sherman

- Leonardo da Vinci

- William H. Johnson

- Tama Janowitz

- Arundhati Roy

- Langston Hughes

- Sylvia Plath

Note: We left actors, actresses, and musicians of the MTV generation out of this section, because then we'd have to include the obvious hotties—and what toiling artist wants to read a list of the obvious hotties?

THE EIGHT ARTISTIC BLOODLINES

Just like dogs, artists can be grouped by breed. The following are descriptions of the eight most common artistic bloodlines. Most artists are, of course, mongrels, and include several if not all of the following personality types. Almost always, however, one trait dominates over others. These characteristics cannot be trained away. The Ramblin' Fool feels called to the highway just as the Golden Retriever feels drawn to the trash can. Each breed suffers its own shortcomings, yet all contribute something essential to the species as a whole.

SIZE ISN'T EVERYTHING

- Picasso, five feet two inches

- Truman Capote, five feet

- The Artist Formerly Known as (and Now Known Again as) Prince, five feet two and a half inches

- Woody Allen, five feet five inches

- Toulouse-Lautrec, four feet six inches

- Spike Lee, five feet five inches

- Danny DeVito, five feet

BUT REALLY, WHAT GREAT PERSONALITIES

- Andy Warhol

- Meat Loaf

- Shakespeare

- Mozart

- The older, fatter Truman Capote

- Bob Dylan

- Roseanne Barr

- Garrison Keillor

Key: The following symbols indicate each breed's disposition.

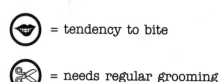 = tendency to bite

= needs regular grooming

 = easily trained

= difficult to train

= adaptable to indoor living

 = happier outdoors

= fox hunter

 = recommended for children

= not recommended for children

 = tendency to run away

INSATIABLE ROGUE

Favorite chew toy: a brassiere

In Woody Allen's *Bullets Over Broadway*, a wife says to her failed artist husband that she could love a man if he weren't a real artist. But she couldn't love an artist if he weren't a real man. Insatiable Rogues are real men. (And occasionally real women.) If you're a sex fiend, dirty rascal, or even just a hedonist, then you're most likely an Insatiable Rogue. The morals of a civilized society do not apply to you: The Insatiable Rogue might find himself accused—justly or unjustly—of molestation, incest, picking an inappropriate partner—take your pick. Your sex drive is spiritual calling beyond the judgment of others. The Insatiable Rogue declares war on any limitation to his self-styled wonderland.

If you're a genius Rogue, then the public might let you off the hook. In *Manhattan*, Woody Allen's character has an affair with a seventeen-year-old girl and loyal fans still praise it without even a hint of irony. Hemingway devotees defend him against charges of misogyny, claiming that his famed heroine Brett from *The Sun Also Rises* was a sexual dynamo rather than an emasculating bitch. Be careful, though, because even the president of your fan club is likely to pack it in when your hand is caught in the kiddie-porn cookie jar.

In much the way that poodles come in Teacup, Miniature, and Standard sizes, the Rogue has different guises as well.

Tiki Hut Rogue Gauguin's trip to the South Seas has been described by some art historians as the mother of all midlife crises. Gauguin, who was known to be both physically and verbally abusive to his long-suffering wife, ultimately left her (and their five children) for the hedonistic pleasures of the South Seas. In Tahiti he married a thirteen-year-old and lived like a king with a harem of island girls at his beck and call. There he had at least three more children, whom he also never bothered to support.

Piggy Rogue Picasso once declared that all women were either "goddesses or doormats."[2] At parties he would walk up to a woman and simply say, "I'm Picasso." When paying for something inexpensive, he liked to use a check, explaining, "People [would] rather keep the cheque for my famous signature than to cash it."[3] In the biopic *Surviving Picasso*, the Spanish artist is portrayed as such a misogynist that a *Rolling Stone* magazine reviewer described the film as "Portrait of the Artist as a Sexist Pig."[4] Yet many historians assert that Picasso adored the women he abused. He *was* very affectionate. Regardless, none argue that Picasso was a prominent player in the Communist Peace Movement which gains him at least some ethical kudos.

Lady Lothario Of course, insatiable sex drives are not the sole province of male artists. There have been great seductresses who reportedly ate up their men, spat them out, and moved on to the next best thing, including Anaïs Nin, Mae West, and Madonna. The popularly acclaimed poet and landscape designer Vita Sackville-West was Virginia Woolf's model for

the sexually promiscuous Orlando. When writing that book, Virginia sent a note to Vita: "It's all about you and the lusts of your flesh and the lure of your mind (heart you have none.)"[5] Indeed, Vita carried on numerous passionately stormy lesbian affairs. When one of Vita's lovers, Violet, decided to get married, Vita showed up at her Ritz honeymoon suite and swept her away to her own small hotel. "I had her, I didn't care," said Vita.[6]

THE CRUSADER

Favorite chew toy: CD of John Ashcroft singing

Without the poets, who would society find to stand on soap boxes and rage against immoral drug companies? Who would slather themselves in black grease for the "Big Oil" dance collaborative, or stage the powerful "Mink Farm Happening" in the park? But you're too busy, you say, and just don't have time to play corporate musical chairs in front of Rockefeller Center. Well, be glad that the Crusaders have time, because without them there would be no *Fahrenheit 9/11*. Of course, plenty of people might like to claim they're Crusaders, but it takes more than hitting the high note in "Feed the World." Real Crusaders are not afraid of ripping up a picture of the Pope or admitting to their legions of country-and-western fans, "You know, we're ashamed the president of the United States is from Texas."[7]

There's a long history of Crusaders fighting the mainstream to make a better future, or in the words of John Cage: "I can't understand why people are frightened of new ideas. I'm frightened of the old ones."[8] The Transcendentalists fought to end slavery and women's oppression; the Woodstockers protested war with flower power and threw sexual repression out the bedroom window; the Dadaists turned straitlaced society upside down, or, as one of its founders, Hugo Ball, put it: "How can one get rid of everything that smacks of journalism, worms, everything nice and right, blinkered, moralistic, Europeanized, enervated? By saying Dada."[9]

Kathe Kollwitz was an Expressionist artist who was rabidly antiwar. She not only made posters for the women's movement, but also fought for gay rights, a woman's right to choose, and better child labor laws. Not so shabby, but now factor in that she did all this before and during World War II in *Berlin*! If the Nazis ever got her, Kathe planned to drink the vial of poison she always carried around in her backpack. And you thought you were a good person for recycling aluminum foil. This is the problem with artistic Crusaders—they make the rest of us feel like slackers. Kathe Kollwitz would argue that guilt is good and it's time the artistic community got off its collective duff. After all, isn't social justice our responsibility?

In 1967 a group of African-American artists congregated in front of a dilapidated building at 43rd and

Langley on Chicago's South Side. Dipping brushes into paint cans, they covered the eyesore with portraits of their heroes, including Thelonious Monk, W. E. B. DuBois, and Billie Holiday. This activist work of art launched a wave of mural painting in urban communities that continues to this day. Many of these South Side painters went on to form AfriCobra, an acronym for African Commune of Bad Relevant Artists, dedicated to fighting racism and fostering art that celebrates the African-American experience.

Crusaders also tend to use costumes to help them make their point. For example, the Guerrilla Girls are an anonymous group of women who take the names of dead female artists as pseudonyms and dress up in ape masks with the goal of "taking back the 'f' word—feminism." A favorite tactic is to create posters, such as one that describes dropping an "estrogen bomb": "Drop it on Washington and the guys in government will hug each other, say it was all their fault, and finally start to work on human rights, education, health care, and an end to world poverty. Got leftover estrogen pills? Send them to Bush, Cheney, Rumsfeld, 1600 Pennsylvania Avenue, Washington DC 20500."[10]

The next time you get *really pissed off* about something, just grab a few buddies, some leotards, maybe a little body paint, and head down to the public square. On the other hand, if you have no leotards (or friends willing to wear them), you could simply stay home and recycle your tinfoil. It's a start.

THE PARTY KILLER

Favorite chew toy: Emily Post's *Etiquette in Society*

As Jane Austen commented on meeting the Denbary sisters at a dinner party, "I was as civil to them as their bad breath would allow."[11]

Just when you thought it was safe to talk about the weather. The Party Killer's intolerance for all things trivial is a force to be reckoned with. Talking about the weather is what people talk about who have nothing intelligent or politically relevant to talk about. An innocent nicety such as, "My, it's been dreary out there for May," may be met with a caustic "Fuck you," before the Party Killer walks away.

Most Party Killers of the past were independent women far ahead of their time. They made a farce of the well-mannered "interruptible" woman and rendered houseguests silent with their radical opinions. Charlotte Brontë was known to cast a pall over entire dinner parties and Mary Cassatt used to bang her fists on the table when people disagreed with her.

The contemporary Party Killer is still most often a woman who knows what she believes and isn't afraid to rock the boat or burn her bridges. When she's had it with the blubbering uninformed, she retreats to her book-lined room to catch up on the important issues of the day, perhaps read a little Proust in the original

French. You're a Party Killer if you've been told at least three of the following:

- "Please, can't you just let it slide this once?"

- "You really think it's worth jeopardizing everything?"

- "Shut the fuck up already."

- "Don't ever come back here again, ever."

Take Susan Sontag: social critic, novelist, and a self-described "zealot of seriousness." She wasn't afraid of getting blackballed for swimming against the popular tide. After 9/11, Sontag wrote in the *New Yorker*, "Whatever may be said of the perpetrators of Tuesday's slaughter, they were not cowards." In a tribute to Sontag in the *New York Times*, Margalit Fox noted that she was described, variously among other things, as "explosive," "aloof," "profound," and "tenacious." But that "no one ever called her dull."[12] In short, she's your quintessential Party Killer.

Another woman who earns the proud Party Killer title is musician Ani DiFranco for her refusal to appear on Letterman after the show's producers tried to strong-arm her into playing something besides her antiracism anthem, "Subdivision." That song begins with the lines: "White people are so scared of black people, they bull-doze out to the country."

THE RAMBLIN' FOOL

Favorite chew toy: LSD
Favorite poet: Jack Kerouac

The Ramblin' Fool can survive on canned sardines for five consecutive years. If you're a Ramblin' Fool, you may find yourself harvesting apples, driving a book-mobile, or workin' for a while on a fishing boat right out-side of Delacroix. You may, like Woody Guthrie, choose to wear all of your clothes at the same time rather than carry an awkward suitcase. The Ramblin' Fool's job is to suck up life experience like an industrial vacuum cleaner. By early adolescence, these artists are already compiling material for their fantastic autobiographies— each day a quest for the ultimate chapter. They can sleep anywhere: the luggage car, the toolshed, the back seat of a Volkswagen. When hillbillies try to beat in their faces, Ramblin' Fools see it as an opportunity to *know* injustice. In their tattered journals lie the collected memories of gas attendants, crazy old truckers, and rest-stop waitresses who taught them about the shit that really mattered. The Ramblin' Fool cares nothing for money—except of course, Bob Dylan, who had no prob-lem dumping his long-fought ideals when Victoria's Secret offered him $1.25 million to use his music in a commercial. Not that he isn't still a really good person. The true Ramblin' Fool accepts death as the ticket to the great beyond. Timothy Leary documented the last great trip he ever took in his aptly titled movie, *Timothy Leary's Dead*. The true Fool is prepared for the other side, sardines or no sardines.

THE MEGALOMANIAC

Favorite chew toy: everyone else

"You've got Gershwin with you," George Gershwin used to remind his chauffeur, "so drive carefully."[13]

Beware of the artist who refers to himself in the third person. This is always a bad sign. Naming six of your male children George, or ten of them Johann—also a dead giveaway. The most famous megalomaniac was most likely Salvador Dali, who made the unforgettable pronouncement, "Nothing is more important to me, than me."[14] Although Beethoven runs a close second—his finest episodes include dumping food on the head of his waiter and laughing in the face of his own audience before proclaiming them all a bunch of fools.

Megalomaniacs might ask you to take their picture, but only after they mess up their hair just right. They may, like Gershwin, buy a machine the size of a Volkswagen to stimulate hair growth. Maybe they're so famous they need only one triumphant proper noun like Jewel, Prince, Tiffany, Cher, Shakira, Eminem, Madonna. Their mantra runs something like this: *I say I'm a deity and therefore I am a deity*.

Ironically, because most other people have relatively low self-esteem, they flock to the megalomaniac no matter how abysmal the deity's behavior becomes. Prokofiev's response to "It's a pleasure to meet you" was simply "On my part, there is no pleasure."[15] Yet they all kept coming back for more.

THE INSTIGATOR

Favorite chew toy: the Bible

Could American performance artist David Blaine be a perfect example of a Megalomaniac turned Instigator by default? In one stunt, he suspended himself for forty-four days, without food, in a ten-by-ten-foot Plexiglas cube above the Thames River. The publicity earned him millions (none of which would reportedly go to charity), while he caused monstrous traffic jams. Critics claimed he was starving himself for the sake of himself. Ultimately, fed-up Londoners started to throw things, such as eggs and baloney sandwiches, at his plastic cube. They called him "wanker" and "Yankee bastard." They offered him money to *just go home* and made T-shirts that read "Twat in a Box." A "Wake David" group formed, whose sole purpose was to keep the illusionist awake for the forty-four days he intended to hang there. The moderator of the Wake David Web site encouraged the public to organize, stating, "Don't shout abuse at David [Blaine] all by yourself—gain maximum impact by tormenting him as a group.[16]

More often, though, Instigators know exactly what they're doing. Take your Piss Christ Serrano, Virgin Mary–

dung Ofili, or masturbating Vito Acconci. This art hits the public across the face like a two-by-four and sends arts councils running for the trees. Here, artists walk a fine line between creating a sensation and making themselves unfundable.

Publicity, even the worst, is an art form in itself. When Yoko Ono performed her "Cut Piece" in 1964 (she invited people to cut away her clothes with scissors), some critics called her courageous for exposing the tenuous relationship between victim and assailant. Others called her a freak and exhibitionist. At age seventy, she recently did the piece again, this time as a widow of a murdered rock star, her son Sean cutting a piece of the dress away himself. Here, the Instigator's work is so poignant that it bypasses controversy altogether.

So if you want to be an Instigator, don't make the mistake of simply trying to tick people off. Pick a vendetta: the Catholic church, the radical right, the military industrial complex, Burger King. If you hang yourself from a Plexiglas cube, you'd better have a damn good reason why.

THE WOUNDED SWAN

Favorite chew toy: own fingernails
Favorite song: "He Cried" by Morrissey

Some artists' lives are so tragic it's easy to see how their self-esteem plummeted below detectable levels.

Let's say, for example, that your father disappeared and Mother was dead before you were even two years old. Another family, who doesn't really like you all that much, takes you in, yet refuses to adopt you. The thirteen-year-old cousin you marry becomes a tuberculosis invalid and takes six years to die slowly on a straw mat. You are so poor that you live for weeks at a time on molasses and bread. Succumbing to your fast-progressing dementia, you die at forty from inflammation of the brain, most likely the result of alcohol poisoning (though some still argue you were simply allergic). Next to your dead body is the miniature portrait of the mother you never knew. This might explain why Edgar Allan Poe wrote about corpses rather than rainbows.

Or how about a father who teaches you to write your name by tracing the gravestone of your mother who died as result of your birth? At nineteen you run away with a married man whose wife commits suicide, most likely because of you. Your two young children die, not long before your poet husband drowns. Ultimately you become an invalid and die of a midlife brain tumor. What's amazing is that despite such colossal shitty luck, Mary Shelley wrote *Frankenstein* and became an important advocate for women's rights.

So the next time you're feeling really sorry for yourself, stop and ask yourself these questions: Were you a disowned bastard as a child? Are you suffering, needlessly, on a straw mat from a curable disease? Did you receive inoculations during childhood? Dental care? Do your parents have at least one picture of your naked baby ass in the puffy family album? If the answers to at least one of the last three questions is "yes," then shut up already. Imagine comparing notes with Poe— how long until he took off his felt hat and started to beat you?

THE FAKER

Favorite chew toy: artificially flavored strawberry Pop-Tart with Nutrasweet

While women are notorious for faking orgasms, artists have been getting a lot of press these days for faking their own performances. It's hard to say which is worse. Compare an artist of such integrity as Sinead O'Connor to one with as little as that quality as Ashlee Simpson. When Sinead appeared on *Saturday Night Live*, she sang not only bald, but a cappella. She also seized the opportunity to further her vendetta against the Catholic Church. Now, enter the plastic Ashlee on the heels of her "Is this chicken or fish?" sister. Not only does she lip-synch her own song, but she lip-synchs the wrong one. Pay no attention to the man behind the curtain.

It's all too easy to sacrifice integrity, but not for Greg Brady. In the *Brady Bunch* episode titled "Adios Johnny Bravo," folksy singer-songwriter Greg is plucked up by savvy record producers and forced to change not only his outfit, but his entire sound. The glittering Johnny Bravo suit fits him perfectly, but the new synthesized echo on his voice does not. "But it's not me!" the righteous Greg complains. The sinister producers admit that Greg was chosen simply because he *fit the suit*. "You want to hear a new sound?" Greg asks. "How about the sound of me walkin'?" Here, the Real Greg Brady kicks some corporate ass.

In 1990, when Milli Vanilli's record skipped during a "live" MTV performance, popular culture was up in arms; the boys even had to give their Grammy back. Now, with the advent of sampling, half-time extravaganzas, and breast implants, faking it seems to be the wave of the future. So what if Puff Daddy changed next to nothing when he borrowed "Every Breath You Take." And Vanilla Ice? Maybe he'll remember to ask the next time he samples a song from Queen and David Bowie. MTV's 2005 New Year's Bash said it all when Hilary Duff's track allegedly slipped in the middle of "Come Clean."

Believe it or not, contemporary American pop, with its flash profit zeal, did not invent the Faker. Bach "borrowed" regularly from Vivaldi, and Goya made thousands doing knock-off etchings of Rembrandt and Velasquez. Although now they are worth almost as much as the originals.

Will authenticity ever completely lose its appeal? Never. After all, art is a fusion of ideas, not a manufactured product. And people really *can* tell the difference. Just ask the fed-up fans who booed little Ashlee off the stage . . . not that she isn't a very nice person.

THE ARTIST AS SOCIAL ANIMAL

At the dog park, you'll usually find a few extremely well-adapted dogs. They're the ones who wag their plumy tails at every newcomer and politely sit in front of toddlers, offering a paw. They never get in fights, come religiously when called, and smell just faintly of vanilla-scented shampoo. They get everything they could ever want from people who enforce rules with proper strictness and big doses of love.

And then there are those weird slinky dogs who run around the playgroup's perimeter with their fur in a ruff. These mangy outcasts are the dog equivalent of the artists who don't fit in with the pack and have temperaments fundamentally at odds with the established order. They tend to run in frantic circles and gnaw at their self-inflicted sores, despite their protective lampshade-shaped collars. So the next time you look at a dog with cockamamy cowlicks and a bizarre glint in its eye, don't turn away in disgust, but rather ask yourself, "Am I like that fleabag?" What you might discover is that you, too, tend to easily come undone and obsess about weird things that no one notices but you. For all these reasons, the misfits should be grateful that survival of the fittest went out with the advent of penicillin.

NOT THE RACHMANINOFF!: BECOMING UNDONE

The average artist is three times more likely to end up in a mental institution than even the people who work at Motor Vehicles. This inclination toward insanity can be attributed to the artist's

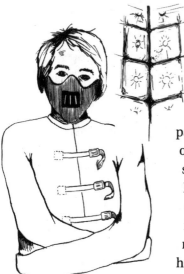

extreme sensitivity. Imagine a crystal champagne glass in a Howard Johnson's dishwasher—this is how the artist feels.

The sensitive artist can tune in to specialized frequencies, not unlike whales, bats, canaries, and certain mutts at the dog park. Artists can go to parties and pick up not only bad vibes, but offensive decor, freezing cold drafts, the smelly sponge by the sink, the glaring halogen light bulb, the fucking car alarm outside, and insulting conversations taking place *about them* at the far side of the room. Other people may need to ingest hallucinogenic drugs to open up their mental floodgates. Not the sensitive artist— for this delicate creature, riding a public bus is more stimulation than the average person might get in a year.

This abundance of sensitivity may be an asset in the studio, but it is crippling at dinner parties, the critique table, the bedroom, the crosstown bus, or God forbid, Motor Vehicles. It all begins with a system error.

First: System Error ⚠ This would include such incidents as the hurling of small technological devices across the room or forgetting to eat for an entire day or having no recollection of where you last parked the car.

Second: Angry Fruit Salad 🖥 In computer slang, this term refers to a bad visual interface design, which can be equated to the human brain prior to snapping. These episodes are likely to include the smashing of valuable objects in the privacy of your own home. Crouched in a corner, such phrases as "I'm such a fuckin' loser" are murmured while sobbing into your clenched fists. While no people are harmed throughout this episode, your pets may be afraid for weeks to come.

Third: Chernobyl Defrag 💥 Here we have a full-system meltdown that culminates with the complete defragmentation of the pixels that used to be your world. These meltdowns usually take place outside the home where, because of your irrational behavior, bystanders feel compelled to call 911 on their cell phones. Most often the breakdown has been building up for weeks before that passive-aggressive Rite Aid clerk forgot, one time too many, to say thank you. Or maybe it was someone closer who set you off— your girlfriend, sister, or mother who simply picked the wrong day to confront you on not brushing your teeth.

When the concept of "a nice little vacation" is suggested, or even insisted on, keep in mind that artists have been going around the bend for centuries. By the 1940s, so many great artists had been hospitalized for mental disorders that artists without "committable" psychiatric problems, such as Picasso, began to hang around mental hospitals for inspiration "to learn new ways of seeing." In 1945 the painter Jean Dubuffet established a new genre of asylum art, which he gave the fashionable name "Art Brut." Suddenly mental illness had some real celebrity endorsement, and everybody wanted to be a nut. Dubuffet did for lunatics what Boy George did for the top hat.

Periodically, artists who weren't naturally crazy enough tried hard to *become* crazy, to "uncook" their subconscious minds. Salvador Dali used to go to bed with a spoon and a dish. When he drifted off to asleep, the spoon would hit the dish and wake him up, and he would paint whatever he'd been dreaming. He also drove around in a white Rolls-Royce filled to the roof with cauliflower, not because *people were after his cauliflower*, but because he was an excellent PR man.

MY DAMN SLIPPERS ARE CROOKED AGAIN: OBSESSIVE-COMPULSIVES AND THE CREATIVE MIND

Chopin could not sleep unless his slippers were perfectly lined up in front of his bed. While manic-depressives and schizophrenics hear voices, obsessive-compulsives just drive everyone around them crazy. What harm was there in Charles Dickens needing to touch designated objects exactly three times (not four or five) for luck? Obsessive-compulsives may be the most tormented artists of all, because it's not easy to pin protective medals to your underwear every morning like Stravinsky, or hold on to your head while conducting *for fear it will actually fall off* like Tchaikovsky.

Irrational fears are often at the root of an obsessive's irrational behavior. Hans Christian Andersen was so afraid of being buried alive that he made a sign to hang above his bed that said "I'm not really dead." Dali was afraid of grasshoppers, germs, being poisoned (his chauffeur tested his food first), and theft. When he traveled he attached his canvases to him with string. Dali's wife found his eccentricities anything but adorable. She finally insisted on living in a castle of her own. If Dali wanted to visit, he had to submit a written request.

Or how about those nutbags we see in the street walking around with their surgical masks? We all know

Michael Jackson's is a lame attempt to cover up his decomposing nose, but E. B. White wore his to ward off germs.

ASCETICALLY CORRECT

Why venture outside the house when your own dysfunctional family is so utterly compelling? These artistic Boo Radleys reside in creepy dwellings where kids dare other kids to go. The house holds some kind of unspeakable secret—a decomposing body or stuffed German shepherd. Or perhaps a pistol-wielding father and a strange sickly child, as was the case for Charlotte and Emily Brontë. Their coping mechanism was to create a literary *Mister Rogers' Neighborhood* called Glasstown.

Emily Dickinson, who referred to her dictionary as her only companion, used to run upstairs and hide if the doorbell rang. She could not address her own envelopes because this meant exposing her handwriting to the outside world. She may even be the only documented writer who had an authentic fear of being published. "How can you print a piece of your soul?" she once asked.[17]

PATH THE ABSINTHE

Few things fill the deep dark hole inside an artist like a glass of pure grain alcohol. The list of artists who have abused alcohol is so long that it would be more informative to compile a list of those who didn't. And forget about chain-smoking, because the same holds true. It's fair to say that a large percentage of artists are destined to become chain-smoking drunks unless they try very *very* hard not to.

Take absinthe, for example. It was wildly popular in France at the end of the nineteenth century because it was far more potent than wine. Absinthe contained a compound called thujone, which came from the wormwood used in distilling the drink and was said to cause not only acute addiction, but hyperexcitability, epileptic fits, and hallucinations.

Several of Picasso's works feature absinthe, but none more prominently than the 1914 bronze sculpture *Absinthe Glass*, which includes a sliced-up cubist body and absinthe spoon (used

for diluting the bitter taste with sugar cubes.) Ernest Hemingway also famously downed the drink known as "the Green Fairy" in Spain and Cuba long after it was banned in France. In *For Whom the Bell Tolls*, hero Robert Jordan tellingly describes the comforts of absinthe as that "opaque, bitter, tongue-numbing, brain-warming, stomach-warming, idea-changing liquid alchemy."

The French poet Paul Verlaine enjoyed swilling the cloudy liqueur and, like many drunks, ended up doing things he regretted in the morning. One story goes that his mother kept the fetuses of her three miscarried pregnancies in jars until the day Verlaine, in an "absinthe fit," attacked his mother and smashed up her fetuses. It's probably worth wondering who or what was to blame—Verlaine, his fetus-hoarding mother, or the wicked drink. Eventually, Verlaine decided absinthe was the culprit—"the source of folly and crime, of idiocy and shame"[18]

Indeed, many agreed with him and an anti-absinthe movement took shape. One of its spokespeople, Dr. Valentin Magnan, the chief physician at the asylum Sainte-Anne in Paris, claimed that absinthe caused sometimes violent delirium—dilated pupils, stiff limbs, "a jet of urine" escaping—followed by bewilderment, as the victim comes to his senses, oblivious to what has occurred.[19]

Another anti-absinthe firebrand, Henri Schmidt, asserted that studies proved absinthe was 246 times more likely to cause insanity than wine. The anti-A movement pointed to the wretched behavior of artists and writers such as Toulouse-Lautrec, van Gogh, Baudelaire, Rimbaud, and our fetus-smashing Verlaine. It was later revealed, however, that many of those who railed against absinthe had interests in the powerful wine lobby, which was suffering as a result of absinthe's popularity. Ultimately wormwood juice was outlawed, although it's now widely believed that absinthe was no more harmful than the common Jägermeister. In retrospect, artists were the ultimate scapegoat for absinthe reform, because so many of them were crazy to begin with.

All of this begs the question: Do mind-altering substances provoke creativity? One thing is certain, drugs *do* temporarily fill the deep dark void. Operative word: temporarily. Is it a good idea to drop acid and attempt to create a masterpiece? Probably not. The work that artists create in mind-altered states tends to be interesting to no one, except maybe that friend who witnessed the melting walls with you. The most embarrassing pages of your journal are certainly those written in the early morning light when you—not yet hungover—

arrived upon the meaning of life. Best to tear them out and start over . . . after you remember where the car is parked.

PARTY TRICKS

All artists should have something they can do to draw attention away from their friends and back to themselves, where it belongs. Hans Christian Andersen, with his excessively large hands, used to make detailed paper cutouts, mostly of animals, while he was talking. Calder used to come to parties with a roll of wire and make portraits of everybody there. Occasionally he would also set up and perform a miniature kinetic circus, which he would bring with him in several suitcases. Georgia O'Keeffe set out to prove that she was more than just a girlie-girl by chopping off the heads of rattlesnakes with her hoe. "Nobody calls me girlie," she once told a cowboy who had committed the offense.[20]

You may want to consider the unicycle or any number of magic tricks. The key is to make sure your shtick is unique—after all, the party moonwalker or beanbag juggler just looks like another jerk begging for attention.

While related, the terms "fashionable" and "artist" are more like an oxymoron when used together. As a matter of fact, artists may be better known for their unfashionable attire. Artists don't get tips from fashion mags, but instead possess a sixth sense. They balk at common trends. No self-respecting artist would be caught dead in a pair of jeans with factory-faded buns.

Real artists fall into what is known in marketing circles as Early Adopters. These are the accidentally fashionable. Maybe you went to the corner grocery one day and forgot to take off your shower cap. A Cool Hunter spots you and photographs you. Next thing you know, your shower cap is posted on Look Look, a Web site that clothing companies pay twenty thousand dollars a year to subscribe to. Within weeks, aluminum mall mannequins all over the country could be sporting your shower cap.

Sometimes being uncool is the coolest thing of all. Rejuvenators bring back such classics as the Hush Puppy, Doc Martin's, and horn-rim glasses by never having *stopped* wearing them. What's cool is the Scooby-Doo Band-Aid on your flute case, or the Boy Scout pin that holds your suspenders together. What's cool is the fashion that comes, unscripted, out of who you are.

If you're a neatnik, your attire should reflect this aspect of your personality:

Mr. Fancy Pants These artists tap-dance the line between dapper and dandy. Some make a dramatic monochromatic splash, like the white-suit lovers Tom Wolfe and Mark Twain (who said his "made him feel clean in a dirty world"). A Mr. Fancy-Pants is big into accessorizing: canes, white gloves, cravats, Panama hats. Dickens was famous for his many rings and stickpins. Chopin had white gloves made to order for his tiny hands and always perfumed his own hankies. Speaking of white gloves, Michael Jackson likes to look like a boy school prep or a military prince. If aesthetic harmony is of the utmost importance to you as well, by all means let your look reflect the unbridled joy of your meticulously organized closet.

On the other hand, if you're a slob, just be the slob you are:

The Fetid Troll These artists are so consumed by work, and they only groom when bribed by others. Hokusai was known to keep patrons waiting while he fanatically picked fleas out of the folds of his kimono. When Michelangelo finally took off his dogskin boots, pieces of his feet were said to have come off with them. No doubt these guys could clear a room in seconds. Beethoven's friends used to steal his filthy clothes in the middle of the night and replace them with new ones. He never knew the difference. And van Gogh was such a pigpen, children used to throw cabbage at his head as if he were a walking garbage can. He once tried to spiff up by making himself a lilac suit with yellow spots. Ultimately, though, he digressed back into the Fetid Troll he was.

A BRIEF HISTORY OF THE BERET

What do Castro, Picasso, and Monica Lewinsky have in common? You guessed it: the beret. The word "beret" comes from the Latin *birretum*, which means cap. Berets made their first known appearance on the heads of European nobility as

far back as the fourteenth century. For a few hundred years, the beret mysteriously disappeared until it resurfaced in the Basque region of France, most likely as part of a boys' school uniform. By the 1920s and thirties berets were common among farmers and shepherds and became something of a trademark of the French working class. Around this time, American Francophiles were converging on Paris, hungry for a foreign identity and all things French, especially the good cheap Bordeaux. The French middle class saw the beret as unsophisticated peasant clothing, precisely the reason expats couldn't get enough of them. After all, most of the Americans in Paris were rebelling against their own middle-class backgrounds.

It's easy to see why the beret (flannel, cotton, satin, or camel hair) has been an artistic favorite. It can cover up your filthy hair or balding head. It can be worn floppy, tipped to either side, or pulled down straight over the ears when the heat gets turned off. It usually stays on when you get punched in the face and it rarely flies off when you're running from the feds. Stravinsky loved his so much he wore it to bed every night, something that Mrs. Stravinsky may or may not have found endearing. He also, as mentioned earlier, wore sacred medals pinned to his underwear—a quirk she must have found harder to tolerate. But who ever said that loving an artist was easy?

CHAPTER SIX

ARTISTIC RELATIONSHIPS

THE RIGHT-LEFT CONTINUUM

Artists tend to be right-brain dominant, which means we're intuitive, ambiguous, and aesthetically driven. Since the right side of the brain controls the left side of the body, we're also three times more likely to be left-handed. This explains why artists such as James Baldwin, Jimi Hendrix, Albrecht Dürer, Paul Klee, Eudora Welty, and M. C. Escher often had ink-stained hands and elbowed their neighbors at the dinner table.

Left-brained folks, on the other hand, think in a more linear, logical, and accuracy-driven way. They tend to work in cubicles and painstakingly balance their checkbooks, whereas righty brains may not be able to even *find* their checkbooks.

Recent studies have also found chemical differences in the brains of highly creative people, including increased seratonin transporters and dopamine receptors. So the next time those lefty brains make fun of you for not having your checkbook, just tell them all about your far superior dopamine receptors. So there.

Brain hemisphere dominance also plays a part in artists' personal relationships. Artists tend to search for that other person who will provide the balance to make them whole. When they're young and romantic (we won't say "naive," but if you want to think it, go ahead), they have lofty hopes of entering into a melding, intertwining, melting pot of perfect love. Not surprisingly, this entails going through many partners.

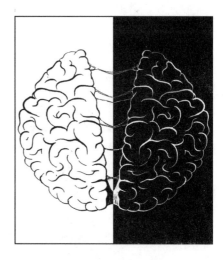

Many, many, partners. Take van Gogh—at twenty-two, the virgin wrote, "A man and a wife can be one, that is to say one whole and not two halves."[1] A lovely sentiment. But after being in a relationship with the notoriously foul-mouthed prostitute Sien, he no longer saw her as the yin to his yang, but rather, "She and I are two unhappy people who keep together and carry our burdens together."[2] Sigh . . .

After a while, it becomes clear to formerly idealistic artists that what they are seeking is not someone to complete them, so much as someone to sit and mock network TV with. There may be no *perfect* match, but there is a wide variety of artistic couplings.

THE FIVE BEST ARTISTIC PAIRINGS

1. LAURIE ANDERSON AND LOU REED: Imagine the Poe-obsessed Lou launching into space with Laurie, NASA's first-ever Artist in Residence.

2. **GEORGE SAND AND CHOPIN:** They were one of the nineteenth century's great gender role reversals. She, a cigar-smoking, trouser-wearing, mountain-climbing, feminist author. He, a sickly, waiflike, temperamental composer.

3. **JONI MITCHELL AND GRAHAM NASH:** "She took me back to her hotel where she proceeded to play music from another planet. I was looking at this woman who was so beautiful, surrounded by these wonderful warm objects, pieces of silk, candles, tapestries. . . . I fell completely in love with Joni back then. I had never heard or seen or met a creature like her in my life" (Graham Nash on the night he met Joni Mitchell). And of course, "Our House" was about their notorious love shack at the top of Lookout Mountain Road.[3]

4. **LILY TOMLIN AND JANE WAGNER:** Jane wrote, and Lily performed, the play *The Search for Signs of Intelligent Life in the Universe.*

5. **GEORGIA O'KEEFFE AND JUAN HAMILTON:** After Alfred Stieglitz died, Georgia spent the last thirteen years of her life with a man in his twenties—said to be her assistant. Only during this period in her life did she begin to wear colors other than black and gray.

THE FIVE WORST ARTISTIC PAIRINGS

1. **TOMMY LEE AND PAMELA ANDERSON:** When Tommy first saw Pam at a party, he walked right up to her and licked her face. They married four days later in Cancun. Rather than rings, they got tattoos of each other's names. Shortly after their wild sex video was "stolen" from their house, Pam filed an abuse complaint against Tommy. The movie they worked on together, *Barbed Wire*, received a Razzie award for

Worst Actress and Worst Original Song. After two children and two filings for divorce, Pam reportedly had Tommy thrown in jail. In 2001 she announced she tested positive for hepatitis C, a disease she blames on Tommy for allegedly sharing his tattoo needle.

2. CLARA WEIK AND JOHN SCHUMANN: When Clara, aka "Queen of the Piano," played a concert, the crowds were so huge that the halls had to hire police details. John Schumann, although a composer in his own right, was generally known as "Clara Weik's husband." This ill-matched relationship is a classic example of a doomed right-brain/right-brain pairing. John died in an insane asylum at the age of forty-six.

3. JOAN RIVERS AND EDGAR ROSENBERG: Edgar was not only a big television executive, but also the punch line to many of his wife's jokes. For example, when Rivers wondered if she was good in bed, she noted that after they made love, "he'd take a piece of chalk and outline my body." Probably the saddest of these jokes would have to be that before they made love, he'd take a painkiller, because a Valium overdose was exactly how Edgar killed himself.

4. LISA MARIE PRESLEY AND MICHAEL JACKSON: What were they thinking? With a span of twenty months, this marriage wasn't the shortest on record, yet it was quick and freakish enough to warrant suspicions of publicity prank. To such accusations the couple responded:

> Jackson: "Just think—nobody thought this would last."
>
> Presley: "I am very much in love with Michael. I dedicate my life to being his wife."
>
> Jackson: "Like we're faking this."[4]

5. **SONNY AND CHER:** When sixteen-year-old Cher met twenty-eight-year-old Sonny, he told her he was a descendant of Napoleon Bonaparte. Cher believed him. She also thought that Mount Rushmore was a natural phenomenon. "You know," Sonny told her, "you can come and live with me because I have twin beds and really, I don't find you attractive."[5] Soon after, they exchanged souvenir wedding rings in a Tijuana motel room. *The Sonny and Cher Comedy Hour* was famous for Cher's exposed belly button and on-air verbal sparring with Sonny always the brunt of the joke.

After their separation, each picked up a solo show on opposing networks—both airing on Sunday evening. It was like the divorce Olympics: Which spouse would be taking home the gold? Cher supposedly won. Even when Sonny died in a tragic ski accident, he was still the brunt of jokes, such as "the most surprising thing about the discovery of the body was that he was recognized."

LOVE PARADIGMS

The following describe a plethora of artistic relationships, beginning with the most creative partners and ending with the least. When a right brain hooks onto another right brain, they're fishing in familiar waters. The further left the artist casts the lure, the more alien the catch.

THE HARUM-SCARUM LOVE TRIAL: LIVING WITH A PARTNER WHO'S WAY WEIRDER THAN YOU

At first such partners can be endearing as they prance around in only your oven mitts and rubber boots. You may shake your head in adoring disbelief as they unwittingly slip into clothes that are not only inside-out, but also backwards. That Band-Aid on their nerd glasses exists not as an aesthetic statement, but because *Band-Aids work really well holding broken glasses together.* You may tolerate their operatic outbursts and scaling of industrial scaffolding, but before long you'll be forced to face some difficult truths: Does one artist ever want to be out-weirded by another? For many artists, maintaining their own aloof oddness is hard enough. Being partnered with someone who is more right-brained instantly bumps the artist one notch closer to normal. Normal, even if it only means "more normal," is anathema.

When does weird cross that fine line into actual mental illness? "Walking to the beat of their own drummer" may in fact be a mild epileptic seizure. Do be concerned if your own antidepressants or Ativan go missing. Do become concerned if your friends continually ask, "Where did you find" this strange new hybrid you call your partner? The following are unmistakably ominous signs. Your partner:

• glues tiny buttons all over the furniture

• harms your animals

• builds a small room in the basement that no one is allowed to see

• thinks you are poisoning his or her food

• paints the windows black

These pairings usually conclude with an agonizing period during which the artist properly dresses and socializes the weirder one, thus becoming a bitter and disgusted surrogate mother.

> **Sex Habits:** "Kinky (pant) and perverted (pant, pant) pant) are *not* the same thing (pant)."
> **Ideal Date:** Chuck E. Cheese
> **Rate of Success:** Not good
> **Pros:** Artist matures ten years in six months.
> **Cons:** "Stop panting already!"

TWO RIGHTS DON'T *ALWAYS* MAKE A WRONG: LOVE IN THE HEAT OF COMPETITION

These relationships are relatively sound until one artist becomes more successful than the other. Late at night, naked and spooned, you might promise each other that all you really want is a little Airstream out in the country. Other subtle lies get exchanged in the candlelight flicker: "You look better in a crew cut—really."

The undercurrent of jealousy and fear of the other's success can remain hidden for years, until one artist begins to get some *real* recognition. This is when comments such as "I'm not saying it *sucks*, it's just somewhat contrived for my taste, that's all" begin to froth from the lips of the invisible one.

In addition to making you feel like a comparative failure, a partner's success can make you reevaluate his or her work. Admiring your partner's work too much can make your own seem shallow and inconsequential. This is bad, but not as bad as secretly hating your partner's work and having to lie each time your opinion is summoned. Better to lie than respond with the opener, "Can I be perfectly honest here?" Going out for a pack of cigarettes and never coming back will damage your partner less than being perfectly honest about his or her work.

Sex Habits: Simultaneous submissions = simultaneous rejections = simultaneous orgasms
Ideal Date: *Eraserhead* matinee
Rate of Success: Not bad if you both remain in obscurity
Pros: Pricing Airstream trailers on eBay
Cons: "Your fucking studio *is* bigger than mine."

ONE BIG, FAT, LOBOTOMIZED BRAIN: TWO HALVES THAT MAKE UP ONE DYSFUNCTIONAL WHOLE

This pairing finds one left-brain partner and one right-brain partner attempting to live together and function as a single, super-size brain. While the left brain is running cost comparisons of all available long-distance plans, the artist is busy wrapping the radiators with Christmas lights. Here there is no competition, no fighting over who spotted the thrift shop bowling shirt first. You are each like an anthropological experiment to the other. Your partner's proclivities are so foreign, so incomprehensible, that they often intrigue rather than offend you. The artist may also become privy to formerly closed geek culture circles—may even try his or her hand at sophisticated word games that involve no alcohol at all. Artistis may find themselves at stamp and mineral shows, chuckling subversively at the fickle winds of fate. If the left and right brain marry, the artist's formerly nonexistent retirement plan suddenly blossoms into a painstakingly researched and well-diversified stock portfolio. Best of all, the left brain couldn't care less about your freakish ceramic clown collection. In fact, it's never even been noticed.

However, as dogs and cats may tolerate and even mildly entertain each other for short periods of time, left- and right-brain partners will often migrate back to their respective homelands. What begins as mild dissatisfaction can slowly fester until one or the other ends up on the back porch late at night, emitting a deep guttural howl. The left-brain partner longs for the geekish fanny pack they left behind; they are sick of defending their coin collection, tired of films with subtitles and "This American Life." The right brain, in turn, longs for the malnutrition and anxiety attacks of yesteryear. They are weary of having their grammar corrected, their mittens clipped onto their practical winter coats. The artist has been to the other side, broken bread with the Vulcans, waltzed with the Romulans, but in the end, must return to their island of misfit toys.

Sex Habits: Between 4.6 and 7.8 minutes
Ideal Date: Splitting up at the Smithsonian
Rate of Success: Better after sixty-five
Pros: You were sick of Kafka anyway.
Cons: "No, Kafka is not a whole-grain breakfast cereal."

THE HOUSE NEXT DOOR: WANTING "SPACE" DOESN'T MEAN I DON'T LOVE YOU

This right-brain/right-brain arrangement has a well-proven track record. Many artistic couples tire of breaking up and getting back together over and over—not to mention all those lost security deposits. The House Next Door exists somewhere between "Get out of my house, you bastard" and "I love you, don't leave me."

With this arrangement, no one has to bargain sex to gain advantage in domestic squabbles. The chaise is where you want it, the ring around the tub is yours. If your partner has already seen this episode of *Law & Order*, well, they're welcome to piss off home and tune into something else. This allows both artists to nurture their selfish little ids. Forget all that Imago therapy crap about *your partner being a mirror into your own flawed character*. This arrangement says no, I don't have to run out of hot water or flip the toaster back to "dark."

When your partner lives in the house next door, you can see who comes and goes and mark down the exact times in a book you keep next to your binoculars. And when it's your turn to usher a "friend" out into the early morning sun, you can be assured you're under equally strict surveillance. Unlike partners who cheat on each other and then lie about it, the house next door provides a cement foundation for a brutally honest relationship. After all, without her own separate house, where would Frieda have gone to wail and cut off her hair when Diego slept with her sister?

Frederic Chopin, the Polish composer, and George Sand, the feminist French novelist, lived next door to each other in Paris. It wasn't that they didn't love each other—he kept a lock of her hair in his diary and she endearingly called him "my little complainer." At the same time, you wonder how charming his whining would been if Sand didn't have a house of her own to retreat to. Tim Burton and Helena Bonham Carter are joined by a new baby and the door that separates their two North London town houses. So the next time your artist partner leaves the toaster on "light," take a good long look at that fixer-upper next door.

Sex Habits: By appointment only
Ideal Date: Blowing kisses over the property line
Rate of Success: Contingent on property values
Pros: Double equity
Cons: Double taxes

FLYING SOLO: YOUR ART IS YOUR LOVER

Many artists believe they are incapable of loving someone else because it distracts them from their work, but the reason is more likely that they're impossible to live with. Maybe that last partner complained about your Leonard Cohen records once too often, or there just wasn't room for that photo of their dead mother because your tiki collection hogged the entire mantel.

Let's say you're lucky enough to find someone to put up with your many idiosyncrasies. The question then becomes, can you return the favor? Maybe things are going along just fine until the dark day when your partner begins to play a *Best of Heart* CD. Or how about that new haircut that doubles the size of his or her forehead? Unfortunately, the artists are so aesthetically attuned to their surroundings that it doesn't take much to deeply offend them. An ill-placed Pez dispenser really *is* more than enough to send you packing your seventies bark cloth suitcases.

The artist is then faced with making a pivotal decision: Do I live alone in a studio apartment at ten dollars per square foot, or do I live with four-plus roommates and split the bill? The choice is obvious, although before long you realize that living with four roommates is actually four times worse than living with your ex. The artist then realizes that the only path to true happiness is living alone and growing herbs out of milk cartons.

Once alone, the trick is to transform loneliness into productivity, or as Beethoven put it, "I am never alone when I am alone." Tell yourself: As a famous artist, I can have anyone I want because fame is the best aphrodisiac of all. Until then, trolling the bars for love takes more time and effort than settling down with your pencil at home. Besides, with the right accolades, you can score partners who would have laughed at you before. Famous artists are never asked to pare down their tiki collections or stop playing the same Leonard Cohen record over and over. Their partners love them for the brilliant people they are—

THE NANNY DID IT

When tragedy strikes, the wailing artist may find comfort in the arms of a paid professional. These relationships give the term "housekeeping" a whole new meaning.

• When Rembrandt's wife died, he carried on illicit relationships with the maid *and* the nanny, both at the same time. His wife's will demanded that he not remarry, but the nanny took Rembrandt to court, claiming that he promised to make her an honest woman. When the court ordered Rembrandt to support the nanny, he had her thrown into an asylum, and that took care of that. Meanwhile, the maid was having his baby.

• After Marc Chagall's wife died, the artist's hair went immediately gray. To soothe himself, he had a baby with his English housekeeper and when she dumped him, he married his Russian housekeeper.

brilliant people with documentation from art critics to prove it.

> **Sex Habits:** The Whippy Pickle 2000
> **Ideal Date:** Reading *Walden* again
> **Rate of Success:** 24-7 is a lot of you to take.
> **Pros:** Four D batteries last a *whole* three hours on Hyper-Jiggle.
> **Cons:** Four D batteries last *only* three hours on Hyper-Jiggle.

A FEW BRAVE WOMEN WHO REMAINED ADAMANTLY UNCOUPLED

• Jane Austen: The thought of marrying made her squeamish.

• Louisa May Alcott: "I'd rather be a spinster and paddle my own canoe."[6]

• Frances Hodgson Burnett: After two divorces, she finally realized that marriage seriously inhibited her work.

• Zora Neale Hurston: She never found a husband who did not interfere with her writing. Her first husband accused her of hexing him with voodoo spells.

STAGES OF ASPIRATION

While the percentage of artists who achieve fame and glory remains staggeringly low, the hope of such a life is enough to maintain an artist's romantic dignity. They are less desperate for partners than other singles and rarely do they partake in ritual dating services. The continuum looks something like this:

Stage 1—Everyone breaks up with me/I break up with everyone.

Stage 2—I don't need anyone or anything except my art.

Stage 3—When I achieve recognition, I can finally score a worthy partner.

Stage 4—I become famous.

Stage 5—The partner/fan of my dreams *finds me.*

What most artists don't anticipate is that the distance between Stage 3 and Stage 4 takes much longer than their six anticipated months. It takes twenty years on average, if it ever happens at all. One day the artist looks down and finds his or her wrinkled hands wrapped around a cat whose ironic name seemed like a good idea fifteen years ago.

You know you're caught between Stages 3 and 4 when:

• the term "emotionally unavailable" has no effect on you whatsoever.

• you have a cat who doesn't like you.

• you watch Dr. Phil with all the shades drawn.

• you think grooming is for chumps.

• you own an undisplayed copy of *The Artist's Way*.

• you have recently upped your antidepressants again.

BENEFACTORS: THEIR CARE AND FEEDING

Love is highly overrated. Benefactors satisfy an artist's deeper needs—available cash and an appreciative audience. Men, don't waste your time prowling around in search of a shriveling, jilted heiress like Miss Havisham in *Great Expectations*. The chance of you becoming the artistic plaything for an embittered, multimillionaire eccentric are not worth pursuing. Should you be lucky enough to be part of the .3 percent of artists who secure a patron (and no, your parents don't count), then it is imperative to keep the relationship (i.e., the paycheck) as healthy as possible. Take a lesson from Bach, who once tried to walk off a job. His patron, a duke, was so beside himself that he threw the composer in jail. A month in the slammer gave Bach time to think about where his next bowl of gruel was coming from.

Being irreplaceable is a trustworthy strategy. Savvy artists woo their patrons, Cyrano de Bergerac–style, to open up their hearts, minds, and pocketbooks. For example, Michelangelo and Raphael were partial to superimposing the faces of patron popes into Biblical scenes (as if no one would figure out that these popes really weren't just *hanging around* in BC times). Bach tried to help out one insomniac patron named Goldberg by writing the *Goldberg Variations* with the intention of boring the man to sleep.

By all means, if you paint a patron make sure he or she appears more attractive than he or she actually is. Learn a lesson from John Singer Sargent, who was commissioned to paint Madame X. In his portrait, the woman's nose was not so much prominent as downright snoutish. Her bare pasty arms hung flaccid beside the sausage of her torso. Society was aghast. Poor John, formerly the darling of Paris, had no choice but to go into exile. Mary Cassatt was also accused of making a patron's nose too "piggish." In contrast, Andy Warhol churned out Polaroid/silk screen knock-offs of fat cats at $50,000 a pop. *Everyone* looks great in high-contrast silk screen. Remember this.

Then there was Diego Rivera, who mischievously put the head of Lenin in a mural he painted at Rockefeller Center. His patron, Nelson Rockefeller, told him a great many people would be offended, but Diego left the head in anyway. Of course, he never worked for

Nelson again, and no mural regales the wall today because it was reduced to dust. Admittedly, however, Diego got a great story out of it, and artists should consider whether or not they want to have a Leninhead story of their own—a great cocktail party anecdote about sticking it to the Man. On the downside, the artist may never work for money again. It's a tough choice. When the artist bravely chooses dignity over financial posterity, the noble act is often referred to as "pulling a Leninhead."

Historically, patrons tend to be art ignoramuses, particularly popes and fascist dictators. Like a stockbroker, the critic tells the naive moneybag what's hip to buy, just like Carson from *Queer Eye*. So the next time some dork with a penthouse asks you to create something "crimson and beige" to hang over the couch, just nod enthusiastically while you imagine Carson and the boys demolishing that couch as well as waxing off his back hair.

THE LAST LAUGH

If the compunction to insult or get one over on your benefactor is too great to be ignored, then we suggest something subtle—something *très Da Vinci Code* involving pentagrams, Fibonacci sequences, or at least bubba talk. Here are some of our favorite last laughs:

• At the turn of the last century, the Parisian decorative Nabi painters turned the natural world into the visual equivalent of wallpaper for their wealthy patrons. Their hidden message? Your obsession with bourgeois interiors has soiled your view of the natural world.

• As Michelangelo was finishing painting the Sistene Chapel, the Vatican's master of ceremonies, Biagio da Cesena, criticized his masterpiece as "disgraceful that in so sacred a place there should have been depicted all those nude figures, exposing themselves so shamefully."[7] Michelangelo got back at Biagio by painting him as the figure Minos, with a snake curling up his leg and surrounded by devils.

• Pieter Brueghel the Elder did a self-portrait titled *The Artist and the Connoisseur*, in which an arrogant patron is looking over Brueghel's shoulder. The artist appears ready to spit.

COSMO QUIZ TO FIND YOUR PERFECT PATRON

1. You find having sex with people in wheelchairs:
   a) repulsive.
   b) not so gross.
   c) hard on your sciatica.
   d) no problem, as long as I'm hooked up to a book on tape.
   e) Fasten that emergency brake!

WHAT TO DO AND WHAT NOT TO DO TO YOUR BENEFACTOR

• Don't participate in sarcastic Billionaires for Bush events.

• Don't beg for more money please, please, please, please. . . .

• Do send homemade greeting cards.

• Do not make fun of their Thomasville sofa.

• Do use sex or the lack thereof as a manipulative tool.

• Do compliment them on their exquisite taste in everything.

• Do not ask for a ride on their private jet.

2. You find compromising your religious, political, and artistic values:
   a) unthinkable, I'm no corporate whore.
   b) a means to an end.
   c) not a problem if the numbers pan out.
   d) a great way to meet interesting people.
   e) I have no fucking values.

3. You find creating propaganda to further an unjust cause:
   a) shoot me first.
   b) unconscionable.
   c) surviving in the big city.
   d) a great bullet for my résumé.
   e) pretty cool.

4. Changing a Depends is:
   a) something I wouldn't do for my own mother.
   b) not so bad when I'm wearing my gas mask.
   c) an unfortunate part of my job description.
   d) a small price to pay.
   e) a fabulous opportunity to further my career.

5. The best place to find a benefactor is:
   a) they find me, on opening night.
   b) the park on Sunday.
   c) museum benefits.
   d) AARP conventions.
   e) near the first tunnel exit.

6. My Absolut bottle would:
   a) include the phrase "corporate scum."
   b) subtly turn the O into a ticking bomb.
   c) be a terrific venue for my work.
   d) feature my best side.
   e) include a heartfelt testimonial about how
      vodka helped me find my "voice."

To score, give yourself:

1 point for every *a*.

2 points for every *b*.

3 points for every *c*.

4 points for every *d*.

5 points for every *e*.

If your score was between 6 and 12: You're most likely to own little more than a flea-ridden mattress and a bread crate for the rest of your life. Remember that Goya beans straight out of the can cause aluminum to build up inside the kidneys.

If your score was between 12 and 24: Integrity is something you can maybe get back to once you've invested your savings in big tobacco. You can now leave the Salvation Army behind and enjoy shopping at the local

Target, where the shoes don't smell and actually match, even though they're made by small children in Malaysia.

If your score was 24 to 30: By all means, open a 401K, because you are going to need it to shelter those taxable earnings. Remember, in insurance language, benefactor also means that line after "In case of death." By the end of your first fabulous year together, every policy should be in your name.

ARTISTS AND THEIR MOTHERS

Ninety-nine out of one hundred artists live with their mothers because they can't hold down a paying job. Mothers who allow their artist children to live off the fruit of their labors are usually of the doormat variety. They see their children as helpless fledglings and jump at the opportunity for a life of shared Shake 'n Bake pork chops. In this symbiotic relationship, the artist is waited on hand and foot like a Southern plantation owner and the mom is assured protection against neighborhood hooligans and overflowing toilets, and help with that hard-to-change hall light bulb.

At times the romantically incapacitated artist will also end up clinging to Mom and the safety of the family nest, as was the case with Joseph Cornell, famous for his meticulous box assemblages. He could have afforded otherwise, but the artist lived the bulk of his life in Queens, New York, with his mother and crippled brother. It's rumored he was a virgin when he died.

Rarely, very rarely, the mother will come to live with the artist. A mother usually shows up unannounced, a bulging tapestry suitcase in each arthritic hand. This was how Julia Warhol landed one day at her son's Upper East Side apartment. Andy Warhol, groovester extraordinaire, had little time to consider the potential humiliation that his mother *just in from Pittsburgh* could have on his Velvet Underground pals. Or maybe Andy was too cool to care. They lived together for years on Lexington and 89th Street with up to twenty cats at a time. Andy turned his mom into an eccentric asset: He worked in an old hat factory covered with tin foil *and* lived with his mother.

Mrs. Warhol was busy searching for a wife for Andy, apparently unaware that he was busy making gay porn films, including the appropriately titled *Blow Job*, which went on for thirty-five minutes. Despite its peculiarities, Andy's relationship with his mother was precious, though few could get him to admit it. As a child, he often made illustrations for his mother's simple recipes. One, titled *Hard Boiled Egg*, still survives. In this same tradition, Andy later asked Mom to handwrite the recipes for a cookbook he was illustrating called *Wild Raspberries*. This book is not only sweet and quirky, but it says more about Andy's relationship with his mother than *he* ever did. And that Campbell's Soup can? Apparently, that's what Mom made him every day for lunch. When she died, one year after she left New York, Andy would never talk about it. Friends would ask about his mother, and the King of Pop would simply tell them she was fine.

James Whistler was equally welcoming when his straitlaced mother showed up in London. A less generous son might have said, "Escaping the Civil War, my ass"—especially since Whistler had to evict his mistress in order to make room for Mom.

"WHEN ARE YOU GOING TO GROW UP AND GET A REAL CAREER?"

One-liners to fire back at Mom:

• When you stop cutting up my meat.

• When you stop laughing at my army boots.

• you stop folding my underwear into neat little triangles.

• When you freeze me out of the (garage, basement, attic).

• When you learn how to use a fucking cell phone.

• When it's time to change your colostomy bag.

Socially, things had been going so well for James—until he had to admit to his fashionable friends (Oscar Wilde included) that his Puritan mama was visiting indefinitely. When the irritated James painted his mother, he named the portrait *Arrangement in Gray and Black*, a title worth a thousand words.

And van Gogh? Poor slob—he was maternally doomed from the beginning. Throughout his entire childhood Vincent's mother was deeply depressed over her loss of a previous son. The child had died exactly one year *to the day* before Vincent was born. His name? Also Vincent. The living Vincent regularly accompanied his despondent mother to the gravestone that bore his own name. On top of this, Mom was known to treat him like an incontinent, flea-ridden mutt. To this day, psychologists speculate that his renowned troubles with women and amputation were directly related to his failure to become the dead brother he could never replace.

SEX AND THE ARTISTIC GUY

Sex has always been a surefire motivator. Throughout the centuries sex has inspired mediocre men to do remarkable things. Even today, the presence of a naked hottie is justified by the words "anatomy study." Art is the best excuse yet to stare at contorted people in the buff. It's safe to say, then, that sex has driven many a man to declare himself an artist. Unlike those who may want to become gynecologists for all the wrong reasons, painters can be any creep. There exists no built-in filtration system for artists, no bar or sleepless residencies to weed out the undesirables. As Nigel Cawthorne puts it in his book, *Sex Lives of the Great Artists*, the female models were often "hookers" on the side and "would be available after modeling to smooth overheated artists by reverting to their principal calling."[8]

Society frowns when a schoolteacher is caught hiring hos down by the river, but painters are allowed a greater moral leeway than the average man. When the artist hires a prostitute, even the church folk don't bat an eye because the prostitute is obviously a nude model, as well as a child of God, and at least she's earning an honest buck even if she's splayed out on a velvet chaise. Gauguin and Modigliani both confessed that they could not paint a naked woman unless they had sex with her. Not a bad deal as far as the penis is concerned. In a short essay titled "Concerning the Rod," Leonardo da Vinci waxes about his manhood, stating, "It holds conference with the human intelligence and sometimes has intelligence itself."[9]

With an untrustworthy organ such as this, the male artist may not be as good a candidate for marriage as, say, an accountant whose clothing is removed less frequently on the job.

Gauguin claimed his talent could not thrive in the shackles of a normal married life. He *had* to leave his wife and five children; "his genius demanded it."

There is no doubt, the artistic dude gets more chicks than

Mr. Nice Guys. In fact, some jealous Mr. Nice Guys have been known to stop bathing and distress their Brooks Brothers leather jackets by repeatedly scraping them along the mortar of their exposed brick walls. These imposters may show up in fashionable bars with house paint dribbled onto the toes of their shoes and an affected look of torment on their unshaven faces. There, they'll approach a babe with the line: "This hole is so po-mo." After offering a sip of their Rolling Rock, they slyly ask, "You got a place you can take me? My loft is being renovated."

As long suspected and mourned by heterosexual women, male artists are three times more likely to be gay, as well as far better looking than their straight counterparts. Modern gay male artists are more openly gay than those of the past, largely because they no longer have to worry about having their hands cut off or being burned at the stake. Statistically, poets are gayer than writers, who are gayer than visual artists, who are gayer than musicians (except for glochenspielers, who are 98 percent gay). Gay art covers a vast continuum—from S&M (Mapplethorpe), to Mrs. Dalloway as a modern-day fag-hag (Michael Cunningham), to juicy soap operas in the Castro (Armistead Maupin). Or just plain old-fashioned tributes to love. Imagine: Allen Ginsberg and Peter Orlovsky frolicking naked in the dewy fields of their beloved Cherry Valley Farm. Other times the muse whispers sweet whatnots in the poet's ear, as on the stormy night when Walt Whitman boarded an empty streetcar and saw the driver studying him. With his gay-dar all aquiver, the poet came forward and the driver rested his hand on Walt's knee. "We understood," the driver said simply of the night they fell in love.

SEX AND THE ARTISTIC GAL

Up until the twentieth century, women's participation in the arts was pretty much limited to either posing naked or perpetuating artistic gene pools. Those who did take the plunge often found themselves committed by their husbands to sanitariums. Their so-called weak nervous systems were treated with the popular "rest cure," which Charlotte Perkins Gilman describes in her groundbreaking short story "The Yellow Wallpaper." The rest cure, developed by Silas Weir Mitchell in the United States in the 1870s, forbade female patients to touch a pen, brush, or pencil and included restricted feeding. The male physician was to teach his "hysterical" female patient that "her supplications are useless, and that she will revolt in vain against a will that is enlightened and superior to her own."[10] Lying in bed, the woman artist could have "absolute rest of the intellect." Meanwhile, she was forced to consume four to five pints of milk a day, with no other nourishment. After a week or so, she was allowed small amounts of meat, more milk, milk extract, cod liver oil, and beef tea.

In Britain the ironically named Dr. George Savage latched enthusiastically onto this rest cure and began prescribing it to his patients,

DID YOU SAY CHANCRE?

As if it wasn't hard enough to be poor without open sores (chancres), dementia, and paralysis. Gauguin thought it was the humid Tahiti weather that was inhibiting that pesky sore on his ankle from healing, but after two years, he found himself standing before an island doctor asking, "You say chancre?" Syphilis was very common among the brothel crowd, which is where van Gogh, Gauguin, Toulouse-Lautrec, and William H. Johnson acquired theirs (though Nietzsche *supposedly* got his from a medical infection). Cellini was apparently in the tertiary stage of syphilis when some of his scorned business partners tried to poison him with mercury. Rather than becoming a murder victim, Cellini credited his assailants with curing him of "the dreaded pox." The mercury treatments unfortunately turned patients a morbid shade of gray.

including Virginia Woolf. After being in his care for eight months, she wrote in her diary, "I have never spent such a wretched eight months in my life." She wondered why Savage could not see that, declaring, "If only that pigheaded man Savage will see that this is the sober truth and no excuse!"[11] When she eventually escaped from Savage's clutches, Woolf pilloried him as the character of Doctor Holmes in *Mrs. Dalloway*, who eventually drives Septimus Smith to kill himself.

My, how things have changed for the woman artist, but just how drastically remains to be seen. Many pop stars cum "artists" use their sexuality as little more than a manipulative tool. They perpetuate ye olde Madonna-whore dichotomy, alternating between porn star ho and naive schoolgrl. These virginal nymphs point their breasts at our culture like loaded guns. "Look away," they say, "I dare you." Bang bang.

On the other hand, we have artists who proudly declare their sexual desires. Margaret Cho ponders these questions in her act: "Am I gay? Am I straight?" She concludes that she's "just slutty." The poet Michelle Tea also provides some eloquent reflections on the matter of slutdom, noting that she had a reputation as a slut even before she had ever kissed anyone. But she knew even then that "being a slut wasn't really about what you did, it was about what you were."[12] And of course, there is the valiant Eve Ensler, creator of *The Vagina Monologues*, telling women to "reclaim the word cunt." Women can have just as much sex as any man and enjoy it even more because a woman has eight thousand nerve endings in her clitoris, damn it! And the penis? A measly four thousand. So girls . . . giddy up!

The female artist, in true rebellious spirit, rejects the sexual mainstream as nothing more than a vehicle to sell more crap to adolescent girls. No good rebel girl would ever be caught dead in a pink T-shirt that read JAIL BAIT. No, she is more likely to dress in layer upon layer of loose dark clothing and sleep with whomever she wants, whenever she wants. And if anyone calls her a slut or a bitch, she can say, with earnest sincerity, "thank you," before quoting a favorite zinger from one of her third-wave feminist heroes.

The power of sex, though, remains a quandary for the artistic girl, especially the ones who want to work in the male-dominated landscape of Hollywood. A Los Angeles billboard was recently co-opted by the Guerrilla Girls (the feminist art organization described in Chapter Five). Above the image of Oscar himself, it read: WHITE AND MALE, JUST LIKE THE GUYS WHO WIN. To date, no woman has ever won Best Director. In fact, women rarely direct movies or television, which is why all the women on TV have their breasts falling out of their sweaters, even when they're in the forensic lab slicing up cadavers.

Women can also make sex a part of their artistic expression. This has been very in vogue of late, with women in avant-garde burlesque shows who declare they are *not* strippers. And then, of course, there is always porn, which the consumers and the producers like to call "art" because it sounds much better than Pussy Fucking Jamboree.

Women artists do not commonly coax men to pose naked for them in their drafty lofts. They are also less likely than the average girl to beg their partners for a marriage proposal. The concept of marriage is often daunting to the female artist, because it involves not only retarded shoes and humiliating customs, but the illusion that a man can and should take care of you for the rest of your life. Though a wealthy marriage may seem a golden opportunity to simply *make art*, the female artist, like a mouse trapped in a cookie jar, gets plenty to eat but eventually dies of thirst.

As for sexual orientation, it's impossible to figure out how many women artists are lesbians, because the numbers constantly shift. After the Lilith Fair has passed through, the percentage of lesbians in any town skyrockets. The fact is that after drinking a glass or two of merlot, women artists who might otherwise define themselves as straight gaze at their girlfriends and think, "Why the hell not?" These women are known to some as "maybeians."

These maybeians may even try to run away, not only from marriage, but from men altogether. The syndrome is something of a wanna-be-lesbian wanderlust, which often includes the mastery of power tools and riding without a helmet. Some say all conventional women have this fantasy, yet only the bravest few act on it.

Unlike these fly-by-nighters, the deep-down lesbian artist never wavers in her conviction and feels secretly lucky compared to her boy-burdened brethren. Some find mainstream success by keeping their true feelings secret and pretending they've got a crush on Tom Cruise until they can't stand it anymore and have to chop off their hair and quit their multimillion-dollar-a-year job in order to be "real." Other artists remain vague. In "Come to my Window," Melissa Etheridge never specifies just who should raise that bedroom pane, Joe Six-Pack or Julie Cypher. Some, like Rita Mae Brown or Radclyffe Hall, send their words straight to fellow lesbians and get intercepted by a curious mainstream culture. And then there are the lesbians who go lavender 24-7, speaking purely to the converted. Poet Eileen Miles described her two-van, thirty-city, twenty-eight-day tour with the radical Sister Spit collaborative as the proudest time in her life being with a group of "female outlaw optimists, teeming with femme talent, total tattoos and fearlessness" and "flaunting a complex sexuality."[13]

BIG FAT ARTIST TURN-OFFS

- saying H*yoo*ston Street instead of H*ow*ston Street

- "A kid could have painted that."

- *loving* Monet

- "You're an artist—can you help me pick a wallpaper that won't clash with my curtains?"

- "That's *so* wild—you should use it in a story."

- cowboy boots

- "Is it true, da Vinci was a queer?"

- Springsteen tickets

- the Hard Rock Café

- "It's not my Durango, it's my dad's."

- fanny packs

- heart-shaped jewelry

CHAPTER SEVEN

ENDING IT ALL

TRACK RECORD NOT SO GOOD

One way to know if you were destined to be an artist is to ask yourself, "Just how bummed out do I feel?" Do you feel as bad as Andy Warhol when he said glumly, "Being born is like being kidnapped. And then sold into slavery." If you often sit at your local dive sighing mightily at the futility of it all, or you get into slap fights with 7-Eleven cashiers, or the word "lockdown" sends you into a cold sweat, a make-believe world may better suit your personality than the shitty one you actually live in. Forget about exercise and eating right, you're lucky if you make it back from the 7-Eleven in one piece. Years of anxiety eventually take their toll, not to mention illegal drugs, cigarettes, booze, falafel sandwiches, SSRIs, and toxic fumes. Your body's something to crash and burn rather than honor and respect.

When it comes to life spans, artists statistically die a good deal sooner than the typical blue-feathered macaw. And that was before AIDS, an epidemic that disproportionately affects people with good taste, fine singing voices, and edgy sensibilities. In his introduction to the anthology *Loss Within Loss: Artists in the Age*

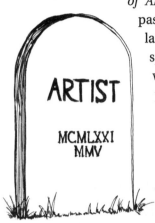

ARTIST

MCMLXXI
MMV

of AIDS, editor Edmund White bemoans the passing of a singular artistic generation: "In the late eighties magazines liked to publish full spreads of photos picturing all the talent wiped out by the disease, but what these photos didn't suggest was that a way of life had been destroyed. The experimentalism, the erotic sophistication, the prejudice against materialism, the elusive humor, the ambition to measure up to international and timeless standards, above all, the belief that art should be serious and difficult—all this rich, ambiguous mixture of values and ideas evaporated."[1] When AIDS stepped in, the discourse between artists and society was tragically disrupted and years of momentum were frozen in place. Society got a glimpse of an art-less world and did not like it one little bit. Or at least most of society felt that way. Jesse Helms might be happier without art that made him think. Or hurt. Or question. Or gasp. Or giggle. Or weep. Or marvel. Or beg forgiveness.

So many great artists of the eighties and nineties, such as the crusading Keith Haring, visionary Alvin Ailey, and rockin' Freddie Mercury, just wanted to live when AIDS wouldn't let them. This may be worth thinking about whenever you ever feel like cutting things short.

WIRED WRONG

In 1992 Arnold M. Ludwig from the University of Kentucky published a survey of 1,005 famous twentieth-century artists, writers, and other professionals. He discovered that artists and writers experienced two to three times the rate of psychosis, suicide attempts, mood disorders, and substance abuse than people in science, business, and public life. Poets, in particular, were eighteen times more likely to commit suicide than the general public. But then poets are also 99.9 times more likely to make no money at all from their endeavor—and while money doesn't buy happiness, contributor's copies don't pay the rent, and that can drag down anyone's spirits.

Dr. Ludwig also surveyed fifty-nine participants at a women's creative writing conference and compared them to the same number of nonwriters, matching them in terms of social, demographic, and family factors. He found that 56 percent of writers had depression, compared with only 14 percent of nonwriters. And 22 percent of writers reported having panic attacks, while only 5 percent of nonwriters freak out on a regular basis.[2]

It's not only the poets and writers who are deeply tortured. Joseph J. Schildkraut, a psychiatrist at Harvard Medical School, and his colleagues studied fifteen different major mid-twentieth-century abstract expressionist painters of the New York School. Based on the artists' medical records, known suicide attempts, and biographical information, they concluded that four of the artists—Jackson Pollock, Mark Rothko, Philip Guston, and William Baziotes—suffered recurring bouts of severe depression. Four others experienced milder forms of depression and mania. Seven out of the group appeared to abuse alcohol. Both Arshile Gorky and Rothko committed suicide; Pollock and David Smith died in suspicious car crashes that may have been suicidal.[3] Some study group.

COLD FEET

Some artists try hard to end it all—then accidentally screw the whole thing up. For example, Goya drank so much arsenic that he eventually threw it up and lived. Others just flirt with suicide as a surefire way to get attention.

• One of Pablo Picasso's lovers, Françoise Gilot, described how each morning Picasso had to be "encouraged back to life." Finally, fed up, Gilot opened the window and said, "Jump." It was the last time he mentioned suicide to her. But Picasso's whining apparently got to his other partners, because two killed themselves and the others just went crazy.[4]

• In the late sixties, Elton John proposed to a woman who didn't even like his music. Realizing his mistake and despondent about having to back out, he considered killing himself. Sort of. His lyricist and friend, Bernie Taupin, found a drunk Elton lying on the kitchen floor with a pillow under his head for comfort and the open oven's gas turned on low. The window, however, was wide open. Taupin wrote the lyrics to Elton John's hit "Someone Saved My Life Tonight" based on the experience.[5]

• Karlheinz Stockhausen, the famous avant-garde German composer, was renowned for such works as *Helikopter-Streichquartett*, which he wrote to be performed by musicians hovering above the audience in four helicopters. When Stockhausen's wife accused him of infidelity and left, he went on a hunger strike. "Every day a telegram came saying he was going to die and that I should come to him," his wife recalled. Indeed, after seven days, Stockhausen broke the fast. During this time, he composed a piece of "intuitive" music to be played by musicians who had also fasted.[6]

THE UPSIDE

There's a reason the "mad genius" has become a cliché. Scientists are now finding that people with a mild form of manic depression tend to rhyme and use sound associations, such as alliteration, far more frequently than patients without this mood disorder. In a 1995 *Scientific American* article, Kay Redfield Jamison, a professor of psychiatry at Johns Hopkins University, stated: "The manic depressive temperament is, in a biological sense, an alert, sensitive system that reacts strongly and swiftly." She noted that the manic depressive reacts to a diversity of environmental and emotional changes. This "familiarity with transitions" is "probably useful in artistic endeavors." In fact, one of the criteria that psychiatrists use to diagnose mania is "sharpened and unusually creative thinking."[7]

But isn't this is what sets the artist apart? Rather than a curse, the artistic temperament has been regarded as the nectar of the human condition. It is a sweet and essential perspective from which to view our often shitty world. Conformists may see artists as a screwed-up sad-sack bunch of people, but the macabre Edgar Allan Poe wondered if "madness is or is not the loftiest intelligence," if "much that is glorious . . . does not spring from disease of thought."[8]

Numerous famous writers and artists—including William Blake, John Keats, Sylvia Plath, and Dylan Thomas—have suffered from major depression or manic-depressive illness.[9]

If you, like so many artists, keep experiencing your share of severe depression, we urge you to hang on.

TEN GOOD REASONS TO KEEP YOUR HEAD OUT OF THE OVEN

1. Your cold-water flat only comes with a hot plate.

2. Think of all the really embarrassing drunken ramblings in your journals.

3. Do you even know how to load a gun?

4. Someone has to live longer than painter Louise Nevelson, who worked into her eighties. And that's okay.

5. John Kennedy Toole threw in the towel after a publisher rejected his novel *A Confederacy of Dunces*. Soon afterward, his mom got the book published and it became a bestseller.

6. What if the Pope turns out to be right after all?

7. Imagine your pet, the only one who *really* cared, waiting at the door.

8. Groupies are less fun when you're dead.

9. Obit will read: "Another starving artist kills self in despair." And you always hated doing the expected.

10. As the writer Dorothy Parker put it: "Razors pain you; rivers are damp; acids stain you; and drugs cause cramp. Guns aren't lawful; nooses give; gas smells awful; you might as well live."

MOST NOTORIOUS ARTISTIC SUICIDES

While we don't recommend it, a disproportionate number of artists decide to throw in the towel before their time. As their tragic final act, they may painfully choose each detail, hoping the world will deconstruct their exit for years to come, that academic papers will be written about why they did it, that shrines will be erected. While sad to think about who the suffering artists left behind, their suicides have become signatures of who they were, and, particularly, how they wanted to be remembered. In "The Broken Field," poet Sara Teasdale aptly described the hopelessness and grief that would eventually lead her to commit suicide: "My soul is a broken field/Ploughed by pain."

Certain artist suicides play out like great classic novels, becoming part of our collective human narrative:

VIRGINIA WOOLF: DROWNING

In March of 1941 the author wrote a suicide note to her husband, Leonard, and her sister Vanessa. Then she took a stroll from her house in Rodmell across dreary farm fields to the dreary river Ouse. Setting her walking stick on the bank, she picked out a very large stone, which she slipped into her sweater pocket, and promptly walked straight into the fast-moving brown water. Three weeks later, some children discovered her body downstream. Right before Woolf killed herself, she asked her editor, John Lehmann, to read a manuscript she was convinced was awful. Lehmann was aware of "an undertow of sadness, melancholy, of great fear." Note the word "undertow."

• In case you're inspired: While drowning does have great symbolic potential, imagine what Virginia Woolf looked like after three weeks in water. Do you want your bloated corpse showing up in the newspaper? Also, your brain can survive for up to four minutes without oxygen. Imagine what those four minutes will feel like.

• Other well-known artists who drowned themselves: Spalding Gray, Hart Crane, Dennis Wilson (drummer for the Beach Boys)

MICHAEL HUTCHENCE: HANGING

The lead singer of INXS died naked by hanging himself with a leather belt. Maybe he intended to do it that way, or, as some argue, perhaps it was an accidental case of auto-erotic asphyxiation. And where was he to defend his case?

• In case you're inspired: When you hang yourself, your bowels tend to release.

• Other well-known artists who hung themselves: Ray Combs, Pete Ham (from the band Badfinger), Richard Manuel (drummer/keyboardist for the Band), Ian Curtis (vocalist for Joy Division, who according to rumor did it with piano wire while standing on a block of ice waiting for it to melt), Rozz Williams (singer for Goth band Christian Death), and folkie Phil Ochs.

ERNEST HEMINGWAY: GUNSHOT

Suffering severe damage to his kidneys, Hemingway had to take meds that sent him into a depressive spiral. In

1961 he turned a double-barreled shotgun on himself at his home in Ketchum, Idaho, ending his life with a blast to the head.

• In case you're inspired: The barrel is cold when it touches your temple.

• Other well-known artists who shot themselves: Hunter Thompson, Kurt Cobain, Wendy O. Williams (from the band the Plasmatics), Vincent van Gogh, Paul Williams (from the Temptations)

JOHNNY ACE: RUSSIAN ROULETTE

This rhythm-and-blues pianist took a five-minute break in the midst of a concert he was headlining with his band on Christmas Day, 1954. Backstage, he picked up a gun loaded with a single bullet and played Russian roulette. He lost.

• In case you're inspired: An empty chamber means back to the drawing board.

• Other well-known artists who played Russian roulette and lost: Terry Kath (from the band Chicago), David Strickland (Brooke Shields's costar on the television show *Suddenly Susan*)

ELIOTT SMITH: HEART STABBING

On October 21, 2003, this Academy Award nominee songwriter had a fight with his girlfriend, Jennifer Chiba, who locked herself in the bathroom. According to the investigator's report: "While she was in the bathroom, she heard the decedent [Smith] scream and she came out and found the decedent standing with his back to her. When [Smith] turned around Jennifer saw a knife sticking out of his chest."[10]

• In case you're inspired: It's actually very hard to stab yourself in the heart and often requires several attempts, what homicide detectives refer to as "hesitation wounds."

• Other well-known artists who stabbed themselves in the heart? There are none; for obvious reasons, this isn't a popular way to go.

YUKIO MISHIMA: SEPPUKU

This is the Japanese practice of ritualized suicide. The practitioner must first write a death poem, then take up a sword and plunge it into the abdomen, slicing left to right. Next, commit an upward stroke to spill the intestines. The final act requires an assistant to perform a near-decapitation, in which a slice is delivered to the neck that will almost, although not entirely, sever the head from the body. On November 25, 1970, Yukio Mishima, the Japanese novelist, invaded the office of a lieutenant general of Japan's Self-Defense Forces, tied the man up, and then stepped out on a balcony to try to lecture the troops about Japan's military inadequacies due to its constitution. When he was jeered, however, the novelist came back inside and committed seppuku.

• In case you're inspired: It can be hard to find a friend willing to decapitate you.

• Other well-known artists who committed seppuku: also not very popular.

SYLVIA PLATH: INHALING NOXIOUS GAS

The winter of 1962–3 was one of the coldest on record, and the poet Sylvia Plath grew increasingly depressed. Her marriage to fellow poet Ted Hughes had broken up and she now lived alone in a small London flat with two young children who were sick with the flu. Low on money, she kept sending out poems, only to be rejected. On February 11, 1963, she carefully sealed off the kitchen from the rooms where her children slept and then turned on her oven's gas, placing her head inside it.

• In case you're inspired: Imagine the grill marks on your cheeks.

• Other well-known artists who inhaled gas: Sadeq Hedayat (Iranian author of *The Blind Owl*), Jim Ellison (from the band Material Issue), Janet Vogel (singer for the Skyliners)

DIANE ARBUS: SLIT WRISTS IN BATHTUB

Her photographs of bathhouses, freaks, and drag queens reveal this artist's passion for the underside of culture.

Even her suicide was rumored to be documented in photographs.

• In case you're inspired: without blood, skin takes on a peaked tone.

• Other well-known artists who slit their wrists or died in the bathtub: Mark Rothko, Sara Teasdale, Per Yngve 'Dead' Ohlin (from the metal band Mayhem)

SINGING NUN: OVERDOSE

Jeanine Deckers, also known as the Singing Nun, hit the top of the charts in 1963 with her single "Dominique," a tribute to the founder of her Dominican order. In the late sixties, she left the convent and her recording career behind to open a center for autistic children with her lover, Annie Pecher. When the center ran into financial trouble, the two women committed a dual suicide by taking massive amounts of barbiturates.

• In case you're inspired: If you don't take enough, you'll end up getting your stomach pumped, and that's no fun.

• Other well-known overdoses: Billy MacKenzie (vocalist for the Associates), singer Nick Drake, Darby Crash (vocalist for the Germs), Marilyn Monroe.

MOST EMBARRASSING DEATHS

Andy Warhol said that "death is the most embarrassing thing that can ever happen to you." This is especially true when you die skiing into a tree or playing electric guitar in the bathtub. The following are deaths that could have been avoided with a little foresight or caution or (in many cases) with slightly less alcohol.

William Holden, actor: Apparently he had been drinking when he fell, hit his head on an end table, and bled to death.

Brian Jones, lead guitarist, the Rolling Stones: Managed to drown himself in his own swimming pool.

Jack Cassidy, actor: Cassidy was the former husband of Shirley Jones and the father of the pop sensations Shaun and David Cassidy. He fell asleep with a cigarette and lit the couch on fire.

Sherwood Anderson, writer: Died of peritonitis after swallowing a toothpick at a cocktail party.

Tennessee Williams, playwright: Choked to death on a nose-spray bottle cap that accidentally fell into his mouth.

Salvatore "Sonny" Bono, singer, politician: Skied into a tree.

Karen Carpenter, singer: Found unconscious in her mother's closet after suffering a heart attack caused by anorexia nervosa. She died shortly after.

Albert Dekker, actor, California legislator: Suffocated, hanging from shower curtain rod. At the time, he was handcuffed and wearing women's lingerie.

Isadora Duncan, actress, dancer: Was strangled to death when her scarf was accidentally caught in a car wheel. "Farewell my friends, I go to glory" were her last words before driving off.

Michael Findlay, horror film maker: Decapitated by helicopter blade.

Jon-Erik Hexum, actor: On the set of the TV spy show *Cover Up*, this actor teasingly shot himself with a blank gun. The jolt caused a concussion, which forced a piece of his skull into his brain. He died shortly after.

Elvis Presley, singer: Died on the toilet of a drug overdose.

Keith Relf, musician, the Yardbirds: Electrocuted himself while playing his guitar. Whether or not he was electrocuted in the bathtub (as many believe) remains a subject of great debate among rock historians.

Mama Cass, singer, the Mamas and the Papas: It was originally reported that "Mama" Cass Elliot choked to death on a ham sandwich. In fact, the obese singer died of a heart attack. Nonetheless, the rumor persists.

John Bonham, drummer, Led Zeppelin: Choked on his own vomit after a drinking binge. Jimi Hendrix did pretty much the same thing, except he'd been taking barbiturates. Tommy Dorsey did it in his sleep after chowing down a really big meal.

Merle Watson, blues musician: Died after rolling over his tractor on a steep hill.

Randy Rhodes, lead guitarist, Ozzy Osborne: Randy and two other band members were in a small plane flying above the parked tour bus where Ozzy was sleeping. They asked the pilot to "buzz" the bus, but when they swooped down, they got too close, clipped a wing, and ended up fatally crashing into a tree and nearby house.

MOST DRAMATIC EXITS

Whether intentional or accidental, these artists went out with a bang. In many cases, these theatrical departures were emblematic of the artist's style. You'll find no wallflowers here.

Elizabeth Hartman, actress: Fell to her death from a fifth-floor window in a freakish re-enactment of her character's fate in the 1966 movie *The Group.*

John Denver, singer: Died when the experimental homemade plane he was flying crashed off the coast near Monterey Bay, California.

Jayne Mansfield (Vera Jayne Palmer), actress: Died in a car accident. Her wig flew off and rumors soon circulated that she had been decapitated.

Jim Morrison, musician: Heart attack while in the bathtub? Or maybe he really was done in by the Central Intelligence Agency or choked on his own vomit? Those who love a good conspiracy theory assert that Jim is still alive and only faked his death. They point to the fact that before he left for Paris, the singer said he might do exactly this because he wanted to travel to Africa and live a simpler life, far from the spotlight. He claimed he'd leave a message in "L.A. Woman" under the pseudonym Mr. Mojo Risin', an anagram for "Jim Morrison."

Phil Hartman, actor: Shot to death by his wife Brynn. Hours later, she fatally shot herself.

Yoshiuki Takada, actor: With the Sankai Juku Dance Company, Yoshiuki was performing *The Dance of Birth and Death* on the side of Seattle's Mutual Life building. When his rope broke, the actor fell six stories, and the footage of his accidental death was shown on the nightly news.

Selena (Quintanilla Perez), singer: Assassinated by the president of her own fan club.

Randy California, leader of the rock band Spirit: Drowned off the coast of Molokai after getting caught in a rip current. He did manage to save his twelve-year-old son's life before getting swept off to sea.

Sam Cooke, singer: After allegedly raping a woman at the Hacienda Motel in Los Angeles, the singer was about to attack the hotel manager, but she shot and killed him in self-defense.

Lillian Millicent Entwistle, actress: Killed herself by leaping from the HOLLYWOOD sign.

FATAL PLAYS

THE DRUNKARD

While performing the song "Please Don't Talk About Me When I'm Gone," sixty-year-old Edith Webster passed out on stage, just in time for her scripted death scene. Unscripted however, was the fatal heart attack that enhanced her performance. Hours later, she died in the hospital.

JESUS CHRIST SUPERSTAR

Playing Judas in a Greek production of the play, Antony Wheeler died during his hanging scene when he forgot to fasten his safety harness. In an Italian production, Renato Di Paolo died in the same scene.

MACBETH

The excitement you feel at getting a role in this play, unfortunately, should be tempered with caution. Now is a good time to take out a life insurance policy.

• Shakespeare played Lady Macbeth when the boy who was supposed to do so suddenly got sick and died.

• In a 1672 production in Amsterdam, the actor playing Macbeth substituted a real sword for the blunt stage one and killed the actor playing Duncan right in front of the audience.

• At an 1849 performance at New York's Astor Place, thirty-one people were trampled to death when a riot broke out.

- In 1937 a twenty-five-pound stage weight crashed within an inch of Macbeth, this time played by Laurence Olivier. The actor's sword also broke on stage and flew into the audience, hitting a man who later suffered a heart attack. This production's director and lead actress were also involved in a head-on car crash on their way to the theater, and the theater's owner died of heart failure during rehearsal.

- In 1942 three actors in one production died, and the costume and set designer committed suicide.

- In Bermuda in 1953, Charlton Heston was severely burned when the tights he was wearing caught fire after accidentally being soaked in kerosene.

- In 1970, playing the lead in a St. Paul production, George Ostroska (thirty-two years old) dropped dead of a heart attack at the beginning of the second act.

SUICIDE NOTES TO REMEMBER

Written in shaky hands, some even in blood, the suicide note is a document sure to get attention. At least the police, if no one else, are sure to read it. Some notes are angry, such as that of poet Vachel Lindsay, who died by drinking Lysol, stating, "They tried to get me—I got them first!" Others are despairing, such as that of French writer Nicolas-Sebastian Chamfort, who said, "And so I leave this world, where the heart must either break or turn to lead." His note was written in his own blood. A few are self-reflective, such as the one scrawled by Kurt Cobain of Nirvana: "Thank you from the pit of my burning nauseous stomach for your letters and concern during the last years. I'm too much of a neurotic moody person and I don't have the passion anymore, so remember, it's better to burn out, than to fade away."[11]

HOW POOR WERE THEY?

If someone stole everything in your bank account and still couldn't afford a Big Mac, don't despair. You're not alone—some of the greatest artists in history have been equally piti-ful in regard to their finances. At your high school reunion, should you pedal your no-speed bike through the Land Rover parking lot, remember: The greater an artist's poverty, the greater his or her integrity. Well, usually. And when the class valedictorian comes over to regale you with heartbreaking tales of her difficulty getting the contractor to finish her kitchen renovation ("and he *still* hasn't installed the Corian counters!"), shake your head sympathetically, then hurry back to the free bar and order something top-shelf. As you down that Cuervo Gold, remind yourself that poverty is merely a symptom of genius.

Unfortunately, the chances of hitting it big while you're still alive are slim, so impoverished artists might want to hedge their bets on posthumous fame. Dream of the day that grad students will spend hours analyzing your choice to cross out "lavender" in that first draft. Bootleg recordings of your earliest performance will sweep eBay at astronomical prices. Well, maybe. Look how poor these artists were when they called it quits:

What were you doing when you were five years old? **Wolfgang Amadeus Mozart** was writing his first composition. Today no one doubts that he was a genius, but during his lifetime, no one saw it. Despite valiant efforts, he couldn't get a nice cushy gig as a Vienna court musician and instead had to settle for being the archbishop's musical slave. The snobby AB treated Mozart like a servant, forcing him to eat with the waitstaff. He was unfit to play in the homes of aristocrats. Fed up, Mozart said to hell with AB and went out on his own. He began touring Europe, but no one really cared. He quickly fell into debt and had to borrow from friends and members of the Masonic Lodge to pay his bills. In 1791 the freaky Count Franz von Walsegg commissioned Mozart to compose a requiem Mass with the intention of performing the piece under his own name. That same year Mozart got violently ill and died from heart failure. At the time of his death, he owned six coats, three silver spoons, 346 books, a walnut piano, and a pool table. He was buried in a mass pauper's grave.

Oscar Wilde's meteoric rise to fame as a journalist, novelist, and playwright was as fast as his fall into disgrace and poverty, and like many hard falls, his was due to a sex scandal. He was ultimately sentenced to two years of hard labor for homosexual offenses and twenty-five counts of gross indecency. All of Wilde's books in print were also taken off the shelves and all his valuable possessions sold. Wilde spent his final years living in a shabby Parisian hotel and intermittently wandering around Europe, nearly penniless. "Like dear St. Francis of Assisi," he wrote, "I am wedded to Poverty." In 1900 he underwent surgery in his hotel room for a recurrent ear infection, and meningitis set in. At forty-six, while dying of cerebral hemorrhage, Oscar Wilde was offered a glass of champagne. His final toast? "I am dying as I have lived, beyond my means."[12] He was originally buried in a pauper's grave, but nine years later a friend moved him to the grand Père-Lachaise cemetery where a tomb was designed bearing an inscription from "The Ballad of Reading Gaol," stating in part, "For his mourners will be outcast men / And outcasts always mourn."

Stephen Foster, the composer of "Oh, Susanna," "Beautiful Dreamer," and many other memorable tunes, wrote songs in the morning, got cash for them in the afternoon, and blew it all on booze that very same evening. One night he passed out and fatally slashed his throat on the sink. The thirty-eight-year-old left behind a change of clothes and a sad little bag containing exactly thirty-eight cents and the scribbling of a new song that began, "Dear friends and gentle hearts."

In her late twenties, **Billie Holiday** moved with her mother to New York and helped pay the rent by working as a janitor during the day and moonlighting as a prostitute at night. She also got whatever gigs she could singing in Harlem. In 1933 Benny Goodman gave her a big break and she started wowing crowds singing with stars like Count Basie. Between 1933 and 1944, she recorded numerous hit songs but earned no royalties. What money she did make went largely to drugs. Despite her profligate ways, Billie did appreciate the importance of money and reportedly kept $750 strapped to her leg in her hospital bed. This was a lot more than the seventy cents she had in her bank account upon her death.

PREPARING FOR IMMORTALITY

Let's just imagine you get hit by a bus tomorrow. Are you prepared? At your funeral, do you want people you never really liked pulling out the Gospel if you've always been a rabid atheist? Do you want an open casket? If so, who picks out your outfit? Is there anyone you would like to ban from your memorial service? What about your obituary? Nothing is worse than a shabby obituary.

You may want to get the ball rolling with the following Create Your Own Obituary:

_____ died of complications of the _____.
   PROPER NAME   BODY PART
An artist of this stature must never be _____
                                                    ADVERB
forgotten. She/he will be best remembered for her/his groundbreaking works titled " _____
                                                        COLOR
_____ " and " _____ _____ ," as
POPULAR TOY   ARTIFICIAL FLAVORING   ANIMAL
well as her portrait of _____ _____ ,
                                FAMOUS PERSON'S NAME   VERB
not to mention the most provocative work, called " _____ Wearing Only _____ ." The
        FAMILY MEMBER   PIECE OF CLOTHING
deceased won many awards, including the _____ Scholarship, the _____
      RUDE NOISE   GERMAN WORD

Fellowship, the prestigious Arts and Letters Medal for Outstanding _____ (NOUN), as well as the _____ (MAN'S NAME), not to mention the _____ (WOMAN'S NAME), along with the _____ (DOG'S NAME). Always a tireless community leader, the deceased volunteered countless hours to the _____ (ADJECTIVE) Children Foundation, and by her/his efforts, made the world a dramatically better place. She/he will be remembered as a visionary, unparalleled by other artists in our time. In fact, they pale in comparison. The city is renaming the _____ (PLANT NAME) Center in his/her honor to assure a lasting legacy.

The artist is survived by _____ (NUMBER) friends and _____ (ADJECTIVE) family, who urge all admirers to contact _____ (ADJECTIVE) _____ (LAST NAME), the artist's deeply devoted agent. A large body of never-before-seen _____ (ADJECTIVE) works will soon be available for viewing, including journals, the artist's collection of _____ (PLURAL NOUN), and several napkin doodles. Services will be held at _____ (PLACE NAME), and all are welcome except for _____ (CONSERVATIVE POLITICIAN), _____ (NON-BUDDHIST RELIGIOUS LEADER), and _____ (HIGH SCHOOL RIVAL). If you happened to owe the artist any _____ (ADJECTIVE) _____ (PLURAL NOUN) or money, please bring these items with you to the service (a complete list has been given to the agent). Also, please note that _____ (RECREATIONAL DRUG) will not be served and screaming _____ (PLURAL NOUN) will be asked to leave.

LAST WORDS

It's not a bad idea to memorize a carefully considered phrase in case death catches you off guard. You may want to utter something more profound than Boris Pasternak's "Why am I hemorrhaging?" Or Elvis's "Ouch, my head."

When asked by her sister, Cassandra, if there was anything she wanted, Jane Austen replied, "Nothing, but death." Actress Tallulah Bankhead's last words were "codeine . . . bourboun." When her husband asked how she felt, writer Elizabeth Barrett Browning replied, "Beautiful." Composer Frederic Chopin pleaded that he be cut open so that he not be buried alive. When Joan Crawford's housekeeper began to pray aloud, the actress barked, "Damn it . . . don't you dare ask God to help me." Timothy Leary was up for the trip, saying, "Why not? Yeah." Acerbic to the end, Oscar Wilde declared, "Either that wallpaper goes, or I do."

Or maybe you don't want to save your best line for last. You might get hit by a bus tomorrow, or you might give birth to the brainchild to end *all* brainchildren. Ahead of you may lie a good fifty years of form rejections, nude modeling, or fame beyond your wildest dreams.

The key is to keep it in perspective—view your artistic career from the bottom up, because no matter where you are, no matter how shitty it gets, no matter how long you've sweltered in a hot dog suit . . . remember, it's the stuff your great biography *could* be made of. And if no one writes that biography, if you remain floundering in obscurity, at least you've lived with pure intentions.

So here's to the artists—without them the world would feel

more like Wal-Mart. Art can transform the ordinary into something more meaningful, even profound. When rewards remain elusive, it's not necessarily because you haven't earned them. The mainstream rarely declares a deserving work a masterpiece; more often, genius is acknowledged only by the truly discerning. It's the protagonist you can't forget, the icon boldly defamed, the scene that stops your breath. Artists are the ones who open the box so the mainstream can think outside it. Besides, what else are you *really* qualified to do?

NOTES

CHAPTER ONE: REJECTION

1. Stone Phillips, "Pee-Wee Herman Creator Speaks Out," MSNBC, April 5, 2004, http://msnbc.msn.com/id/4653913/ (accessed January 2, 2005).

2. Walt Whitman, "Walt Whitman and His Poems," *United States Review*, September 1855, 205–12, http://www.whitmanarchive.org/archive1/works/leaves/1855/reviews/usreview.html (accessed January 2, 2005).

3. Maya Schenwar, "Once Upon an Election," *The Phoenix Online*, January 20, 2005, http://phoenix.swarthmore.edu/2005-01-20/opinions/14537 (accessed January 2, 2005).

4. Alan Smithee, Review of Muammar Qauddafi, *Escape to Hell and Other Stories*, Amazon.com, http://www.amazon.com/exec/obidos/ASIN/276040613X/ref=sib_rdr_dp/104-1185883-0154332 (accessed January 2, 2005).

5. Alfred Armstrong, Review of Benito Mussolini's *The Cardinal's Mistress*, http://www.oddbooks.co.uk/oddbooks/musso.html (accessed February 3, 2005).

6. Harold Schechter and David Everitt, *A to Z Encyclopedia of Serial Killers*, (New York: Pocket Books, 1996), pp. 14–15.

7. Ibid., 14–15.

CHAPTER TWO: THE TRUTH ABOUT CRITIQUES

1. "The Artist, the Critic, and a War of Words," *Observer*, August 17, 2003, http://observer.guardian.co.uk/uk_news/story/0,6903,1020323,00.html (accessed February 2, 2005).

2. "Schneider Blasts 'Pompous' Movie Critic," SF Gate.com, February 8, 2005, http://www.sfgate.com/cgi-bin/article.cgi?file=/gate/archive /2005/02/08/ddish.DTL (accessed February 4, 2005).

3. "The Correspondence," Centre for Whistler Studies Web site, http://www.whistler.arts.gla.ac.uk/biog/Hame_PG.htm (accessed February 5, 2005).

4. Mark Carkeet, "Another Waugh Brings Up a Century," *Eureka Street: A Magazine of Public Affairs, the Arts, and Theology* Web site, http://www.eurekastreet.com.au/articles/0311carkeet.html (accessed February 4, 2005).

5. Giles Hugo, "Road Gang Still Leads the Pack," The Write Stuff, http://www.the-write-stuff.com.au/archives/vol-1/reviews /good-blonde.html (accessed February 3, 2005).

6. Dave Simpson, "Whose Line Is It Anyway?" *The Guardian*, August 24, 2000, http://www.guardian.co.uk/arts/story/0,3604,357988,00.html (accessed February 4, 2005).

7. D. T. Max, "The Critic in Exile," *New York Times Magazine*, January 14, 2001, http://partners.nytimes.com/library/magazine/home /20010114mag-hughes.html (accessed February 4, 2005).

8. Laura Kipnis, "Peck the Knife," *Slate*, July 7, 2004, http://slate.msn.com/id/2103511/ (accessed February 5, 2005).

9. Elizabeth Judd, "Jo-Jo Fries and New Age Dogs," *New York Times Book Review*, Sunday February 27, 2005, p. 12.

10. Notable Quotes Web site, http://www.urizone.net/Olio/Quote.htm, also in many other places (accessed February 5, 2005).

11. Ralph Keyes, *The Writer's Book of Hope* (New York: Henry Holt and Company, 2003), p. 142.

12. Michael Billington, "We Will Not Be Muzzled," *The Guardian*, June 28, 2000, http://www.guardian.co.uk/arts/story/0,3604,337230,00.html (accessed February 5, 2005).

13. Michael Coren, "Greek Fire," *National Review*, September 3, 1990, http://www.findarticles.com/p/articles/mi_m1282/is_n17_v42/ai _8809166 (accessed February 6, 2005).

14. "Catwoman, 2004," Rottentomatoes.com, http://www.rottentomatoes.com /m/catwoman/ (accessed February 6, 2005).

15. "Alexander, 2004," Rottentomatoes.com, http://www.rottentomatoes .com/m/alexander/ (accessed February 6, 2005).

16. "Surviving Christmas, 2004," Rottentomatoes.com, http://www.rottentomatoes.com/m/surviving_christmas/ (accessed February 7, 2005).

CHAPTER THREE: DAY JOBS

1. George Bernard Shaw, *Man and Superman*, Bartleby.com: Great Books Online, http://72.14.207.104/search?q=cache:5wp8oapuuKgJ:bartleby .school.aol.com/157/1.html+%22The+true+artist+will+let+his+wife +starve%22++Man+and+Superman&hl=en (accessed May 25, 2005).

2. 2004 Entrepreneur.com, "25 Part-Time Businesses to Start Today!" *Business Start-Ups Magazine*, http://www.entrepreneur.com/article /0,4621,268741,00.html (accessed May 25, 2005).

3. "Louisa May Alcott," Louisa May Alcott Memorial Association Web site, http://www .louisamayalcott.org/louisamaytext.html (accessed February 8, 2005).

4. "Booklist Adult, v. 99" (review of *Zora Neale Hurston: A Life in Letters*), *Booklist* magazine, October 15, 2002, http://archive.ala.org /booklist/v99/oc2/24hurston.html (accessed February 8, 2005).

5. Kathleen Krull, *Lives of the Musicians: Good Times, Bad Times (and What the Neighbors Thought)* (San Diego, CA: Harcourt Inc., Publishers, 1993), p. 34.

6. Judd Tully, "A Killing in Art," Artery: The AIDS Art Forum, http://www .artistswithaids.org/artery/centerpieces/centerpieces_killing.html (accessed February 9, 2005).

7. Susan Wyndham, "Written into the Vision Splendid," *Sydney Morning Herald*, March 6, 2005, http://www.smh.com.au/news/Arts/Written-into -the-vision-splendid/2005/03/07/1110044253467.html?oneclick=true (accessed February 9, 2005).

CHAPTER FOUR: ARTISTIC DWELLINGS

1. "For Vincent van Gogh, the Work was Paramount," *The Sunday Times*, December 10, 1996, http://www.limrichard.com/arc1984-1996 /arch_c3-101196.htm (accessed February 10, 2005).

2. Ghost Ranch Web site, http://64.233.161.104/search?q=cache :310SQS5tdeQJ:www.ghostranch.org/about/index.php++Rancho +de+la+Burros&hl=en (accessed February 11, 2005).

3. Ibid.

4. "Amedeo Modigiliani," Jewish Virtual Library Web site, http://www .jewishvirtuallibrary.org/jsource/biography/modigliani.html (accessed February 12, 2005).

5. Quentin Bell and Virginia Nicholson, *Charleston: A Bloomsbury House and Garden*, (London: Frances Lincoln, 1997), p. 14.

6. Ben Mallalieu, "Art and Illusion," *The Guardian*, August 10, 2002, http://travel.guardian.co.uk/cities/story/0,7450,772013,00.html (accessed February 13, 2005).

7. The Tahiti Traveler, "Tahiti and Partners," The Tahiti Traveler, http://www .thetahititraveler.com/general/artsculp.asp (accessed May 26, 2005).

CHAPTER FIVE: ARTISTIC STYLE

1. Quotations Page, http://www.quotationspage.com/quote/11721.html (accessed February 14, 2005).

2. Ingo F. Walther, "Pablo Picasso and Women," Artelino, http://www .artelino.com/articles/picasso.asp (accessed February 14, 2005).

3. Robert Hughes, "The Time 100: Pablo Picasso," *Time*, http://www.time.com /time/time100/artists/profile/picasso.html (accessed February 15, 2005).

4. "Surviving Picasso," RollingStone.com, http://www.rollingstone.com /reviews/movie/_/id/5948791 (accessed May 26, 2005).

5. Victoria Glendinning, *Vita: A Biography* (New York: Quill, 1983), p. 181.

6. Ibid.

7. "Chicks' Critical Remarks about Bush Stir up Controversy," Associated Press, March 14, 2003, http://www.foxnews.com/story /0,2933,81093,00.html (accessed February 16, 2005).

8. Famous Quotations, http://www.famous-quotations.com/asp /cquotes.asp?category=Creativity+%2F+Ideas&curpage=2 (accessed February 17, 2005).

9. "Electro-Acoustic Music: A Concise Interactive History: Dadaism," http://www-camil.music.uiuc.edu/Projects/EAM/Dadaism.html (accessed February 20, 2005).

10. Guerrilla Girls Web site, http://www.guerrillagirls.com/posters /voiceestrogen.shtml (accessed February 20, 2005).

11. "The Astoft Collection: Denbary Sisters," http://64.233.161.104 /search?q=cache:2CKJRvzmXXOJ:astoft.co.uk/debary.htm+l+was+as +civil+to+them+as+their+bad+breath+would+allow&hl=en (accessed February 18, 2005).

12. Margalit Fox, "Susan Sontag, Social Critic with Verve, Dies at 71," *New York Times*, December 28, 2004, http://www.nytimes.com/2004/12/28 /books/28cnd-sont.html?ex=1112590800&en=26e93c5fea0fa53b&ei =5070&oref=login (accessed February 21, 2005).

13. Kathleen Krull, *Lives of the Musicians: Good Times, Bad Times (and What the Neighbors Thought)* (San Diego: Harcourt Inc., Publishers, 1993), p. 89.

14. Kathleen Krull, *Lives of the Writers: Comedies, Tragedies (and What the Neighbors Thought)* (San Diego: Harcourt Inc., Publishers, 1994), p. 77.

15. Ibid., 83.

16. "Wake David," http://www.wakedavid.co.uk (accessed February 21, 2005).

17. Kathleen Krull, *Lives of the Writers: Comedies, Tragedies (and What the Neighbors Thought)* (Harcourt Inc., Publishers, 1994), p. 51.

18. The Virtual Absinthe Museum, http://www.oxygenee.com/absintheFAQ5 .html (accessed February 22, 2005).

19. Ibid.

20. Krull, *Writers*, p. 70.

CHAPTER SIX: ARTISTIC RELATIONSHIPS

1. Nigel Cawthorne, *Sex Lives of the Great Artists* (London: Prion, 1998), p. 3.

2. Ibid., 7.

3. "Joni Mitchell: On a Life in Music," NPR: Fresh Air, http://www.npr.org /templates/story/story.php?storyId=4118493 (accessed February 23, 2005).

4. "She's Out of his Life: Lisa Marie Presley Files for Divorce from Michael Jackson," CNN http://www.cnn.com/US/9601/jacko_presley/ (accessed February 24, 2005).

5. "Cher: Eulogy for Sonny Bono," http://www.americanrhetoric.com /speeches/chereulogytosonnybono.htm (accessed February 25, 2005).

6. Kathleen Krull, *Lives of the Writers: Comedies, Tragedies (and What the Neighbors Thought)* (Harcourt Inc., Publishers, 1994), p. 54.

7. Imogene Tilden, "Michelangelo," Guardian Unlimited, July 11, 2001, http://www.guardian.co.uk/netnotes/article/0,6729,520141,00.html (accessed February 26, 2005).

8. Cawthorne, *Sex Lives*, p. vii.

9. Ibid., 36.

10. Hermione Lee, *Virginia Woolf* (London: Chatto & Windus, 1996), p. 183.

11. Ibid., 184.

12. Sister Spit Web site, http://www.klever.org/spit/ladies.html (accessed February 28, 2005).

13. Ibid.

CHAPTER SEVEN: ENDING IT ALL

1. Edmund White, *Loss within Loss: Artists in the Age of AIDS* (Madison: University of Wisconsin Press, 2001).

2. William R. Corliss, "Madness and Creativity Revisited,"

3. "Creativity's Melancholy Canvas," *Science News*, Vol 145, p. 302, http://mv.lycaeum.org/M2/creativ2.html (accessed March 5, 2005).

4. John Whitley, "Life with Pablo was a Bullfight!" *London Telegraph*, September 27, 1998 http://www.suntimes.co.za /1998/09/27/lifestyle/life01.htm (accessed March 6, 2005).

5. "Elton John FAQ," http://www.eltonlinks.com/faq.html#qa4, also in Margaret Moser and Bill Crawford, *Rock Stars Do the Dumbest Things*, (Renaissance E-Books, 1998).

6. John O'Mahony, "The Sound of Discord," *The Guardian,* September 29, 2001, http://www.guardian.co.uk/saturday_review/story/0,3605,559766,00.html (accessed March 10, 2005).

7. Kay Redfield Jamison, "Manic-Depressive Illness and Creativity," *Scientific American*, February 1995, vol. 272.

8. Ibid.

9. Kay Redfield Jamison, *Touched with Fire: Manic-Depressive Illness and the Artistic Temperament,* (New York: Free Press, 1996).

10. "Elliott Smith Coroner's Report Posted Online," *Pitchfork*, January 12, 2004, http://www.pitchforkmedia.com/news/04-01/12.shtml (accessed March 19, 2005).

11. Kurt Cobain, Kurt Cobain: The Note Web site, http://www.hotshotdigital.com /WellAlwaysRemember.2/KurtCobainNote.html (accessed March 23, 2005).

12. Lyle Larsen, "Last Words of Famous Authors," http://homepage.smc.edu/larsen _lyle/last_words_of_famous_authors.htm (accessed March 23, 2005).

LAURIE LINDOP has published eight nonfiction young adult books; her short stories have appeared in *Redbook*, the *Beloit Fiction Journal*, and the *Paterson Literary Review*.

MARIANNE TAYLOR has published short stories in the *Boston Review*, *Sideshow*, the *Southern Anthology*, and many others. In 2005 she won the *Ms.* magazine fiction contest. They both live in the Boston area.